2/17 04

(Memory Shop)

THE ALFRED HITCHCOCK ALBUM

by Michael Haley

PRENTICE-HALL, INC.
Englewood Cliffs, N.J., 07632

Book Designer: Linda Huber
Art Director: Hal Siegel

Photo on title page courtesy of The Museum of
Modern Art/Film Stills Archive

Address inquiries to Prentice-Hall, Inc.,
Englewood Cliffs, N.J. 07632
Printed in the United States of America
Prentice-Hall International, Inc., London
Prentice-Hall of Australia, Pty. Ltd., Sydney
Prentice-Hall of Canada, Ltd., Toronto
Prentice-Hall of India Private Ltd., New Delhi
Prentice-Hall of Japan, Inc., Tokyo
Prentice-Hall of Southeast Asia Pte. Ltd., Singapore
Prentice-Hall of Southeast Asia, Pte. Ltd., Singapore
Whitehall Books Limited, Wellington, New Zealand

10   9   8   7   6   5   4   3   2   1

Library of Congress Cataloging in Publication Data
Haley, Michael.
The Alfred Hitchcock album.
Filmography: p.
Bibliography: p.
Includes index.
1. Hitchcock, Alfred, 1899-1980. 2. Moving-picture
producers and directors—United States—Biography.
3. Moving-picture producers and directors—Great Britain—
Biography. I. Title.
PN1998.A3H5472   1981   791.43'0233'0924   [B]   81-5894
ISBN 0-13-021469-8   AACR2
ISBN 0-13-021451-5 {PBK.}

For Jack Hyde and Janan

Acknowledgments

I would like to express my sincerest thanks to the many people who assisted me in this effort. My gratitude to EMI Films Limited; The Rank Organization Limited; Mark Ricci of the Memory Shop; Mary Corliss of the Museum of Modern Art; the staff of The National Film Archive, The British Film Institute; Cinemabilia, Inc.; the Lincoln Center Library for the Performing Arts; United Press International, Inc.; Greg Radtke; Faith Witryol; Michael Andaloro; and John and Mickey Gordon.

    A special thanks to Tony Paradise for being there, no matter what.

(The Museum of Modern Art/Film Stills Archive)

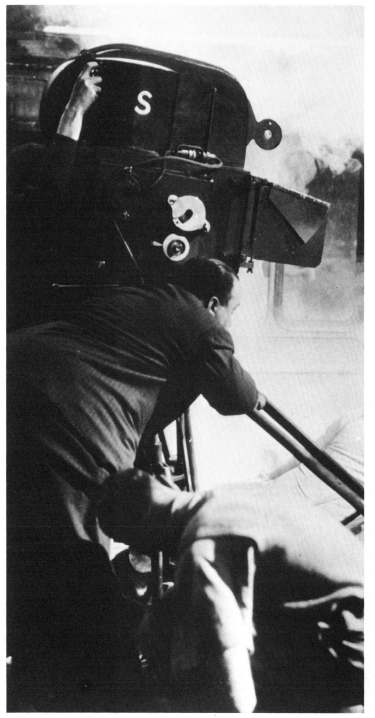

(The Rank Organization Limited)

Contents

The Album

"Drama is life with the dull bits left out."—*Alfred Hitchcock*

In January of 1980, Alfred Joseph Hitchcock was made a knight commander to Her Majesty, Queen Elizabeth II. In a brief ceremony at the commissary of Universal City Studios, he received formal notification. Although he was very ill at the time, he willingly allowed the gathering of reporters to ask a few questions, and one reporter asked if he knew why the honor was so long in coming. After his customary withering pause, Sir Alfred, with calculated brevity, stated his case: "I suppose it was a matter of carelessness."

Carelessness, indeed. Rest assured that if circumstances had been different —that if by some Hitchcockian plot twist this gentle, portly son of a London greengrocer had somehow ascended the British throne—carelessness would have been the last thing anyone would have observed. Sir Alfred Hitchcock was a monarch in another realm, presiding for more than five decades over one of the great artistic and financial kingdoms in the history of filmmaking. With his peppery wit and unmistakable profile as trademarks, Alfred Hitchcock amassed a legacy of fifty-three feature films and an estate valued at millions of dollars. This prolific and illustrious career was handled carefully, with the meticulous attention to detail that became the hallmark of the films of one of Hollywood's most popular directors.

On April 29, 1980, Hitchcock—80 —died in his home in Los Angeles from the complications of many long-suffered ailments. It was a quiet, dignified end to a quiet, dignified life. His wife of fifty-three years, Alma, and his daughter and three grandchildren were present. The next night, on the syndicated CBS radio news report, the announcer bor-rowed an overtone from the master himself, and in doing so, imparted an appropriate farewell: "He died yesterday, apparently of natural causes." That subtle hint at foul play would have warmed Hitchcock's filmmaker's heart.

After all the honors, the kudos from his colleagues, and the praise of his fans, Hitchcock means more than just another film director. It became a word synonymous with suspense—skillful murders and hidden bombs, and neatly textured characters disturbingly like ourselves. It is hard to believe that his magic profile will no longer appear in a new thriller, that there will be no more of the gripping entertainments that were so uniquely . . . Hitchcockian. Somehow we expected him to live forever. With Hitchcock it seemed almost possible.

He was a quiet, simple man of refined good manners and demure English tastes. He eschewed the Holly-wood high life, yet he had a keen sense of public relations. He enjoyed enormous political power over his movies, but often refused to wield it. He loved creat-ing suspense for others, but couldn't endure it himself. Finally, with the ironic twist of a Hitchcock ending, he was a profoundly popular director whose films were critically acclaimed, and yet he personally never received an Oscar as best director.

The hesitancy of his peers to confer artistic recognition on him was partly due to his immense popularity. For some reason, if the public liked something too much, the critics used to assume it must not be an "artistic" work. Nevertheless, as the years went by, Hitchcock began to receive his long-overdue recognition. The Academy of Motion Picture Arts and Sciences nom-inated him for five Oscars for best director: *Rebecca* in 1940, *Lifeboat* in

1943, *Spellbound* in 1945, *Rear Window* in 1954, and *Psycho* in 1960. Then, in 1967, he received the coveted Irving G. Thalberg Memorial Award. This was only one of many honors he accumulated in the twilight of his career.

One of his finest hours came on April 29, 1974, when the Film Society of Lincoln Center honored Hitchcock with a nationally televised gala evening. A glittering array of several hundred of Hollywood's greatest stars and most important executives presented themselves in his honor as he delightedly escorted Princess Grace of Monaco—one of his former leading ladies, Grace Kelly—to the dais. After the presentation of a montage of Hitchcock film highlights, the esteemed director appeared in a response filmed earlier because of his health. The text is reprinted in full on these pages to present one of his most often quoted passages on the subject of murder, written by Thomas De Quincey. His own inimitable closing line will leave you thinking.

"Good Evening. They say that when a man drowns, his entire life flashes before his eyes. I am indeed fortunate for having just had that same experience without even getting my feet wet.

"First of all, I wish to express my deep satisfaction for this honor. It makes me feel very proud indeed.

"As you will have seen, murder seems to be the prominent theme. As I do not approve of the current wave of violence that we see on our screens, I have always felt that murder should be treated delicately. And, in addition to that, with the help of television, murder should be brought into the home where it rightly belongs.

"Some of our most exquisite murders have been domestic; performed with tenderness in simple, homey places like the kitchen table or the bathtub. Nothing is more revolting to my sense of decency than the underworld thug who is able to murder anyone—even people to whom he has not been properly introduced.

"After all, I'm sure you will agree that murder can be so much more charming and enjoyable, even for the victim, if the surroundings are pleasant and the people involved are ladies and gentlemen like yourselves.

"Finally, I think I can best describe the insidious effect of murder on one's character by reading a paragraph from Thomas De Quincey's delightful essay, 'Murder As One of the Fine Arts.' He said, 'If once a man indulges himself in murder, very soon he comes to think little of robbing, and from robbing he comes next to drinking and Sabbath-breaking, and from that to incivility and procrastination. Once begun on this downward path you never know where you are to stop. Many a man dates his ruin from some murder or other that perhaps he thought little of at the time.'

"They tell me that a murder is committed every minute, so I don't want to waste any more of your time. I know you want to get to work.

"Thank you."

And there were other honors. He received honorary doctoral degrees from the University of California and Santa Clara University. The Hollywood Foreign Press Association presented him with their Cecil B. DeMille Award. The French Cinémathèque made him a Knight of the Legion of Honour. In 1969 he was named an officer of the French Order of Arts and Letters, and in 1976 he became a commander of the Order.

The barrage of laurels was in many ways a curious blend of afterthought and praise on the part of those who for

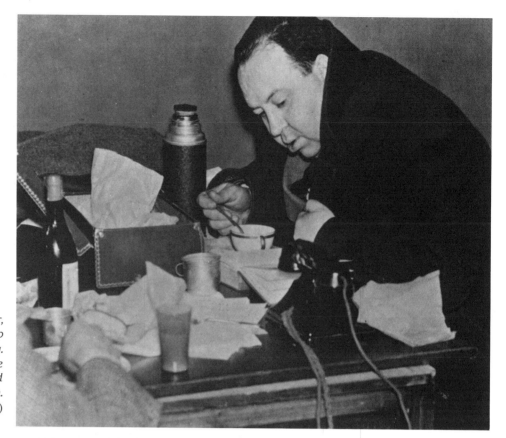

Starting out as a title-card designer, Hitchcock worked his way up by listening and learning. Chilly lunches, like this one on the set of The 39 Steps, *would soon be behind him.*
(The Rank Organization Limited)

many years did not find Hitchcock's films artistic. Detractors abound in the Hitchcock legend—and often rightly so. He was not the most consistent of talents. Considered by many to be the high points of his career, such films as *The Lodger* in 1926, *The 39 Steps* in 1935, *Strangers on a Train* in 1951, and *North by Northwest* in 1959 had counterparts which even Hitchcock acknowledged as "unmitigated disasters." *Champagne* in 1928, *Waltzes From Vienna* in 1933, *Mr. and Mrs. Smith* in 1941, and *Topaz* in 1969 are Hitchcock off his mark. Such efforts confounded even his most ardent admirers. Nonetheless, they would go to remarkable lengths to defend him, to the point of

Soon, success struck with The Lodger, *his classic silent. Perhaps this publicity shot was meant to show the tough side of the budding young genius.*
(The Rank Organization Limited)

saying, "Even *bad* Hitchcock is better than *no* Hitchcock."

Even in his lesser films, his technical skills at moviemaking have moments of sublime genius—or at least flashes of remarkable talent. More important, the nature of his failures offer clues to an ignored quality—Hitchcock's immense humanity. He was a man of certain frailty and vulnerability. Once asked if he scared easily, he replied, "Very. Here's a list in order of adrenal production: One, little children; Two, policemen; Three, high places; Four, that my next picture won't be as good as the last."

In many ways, it is this vulnerable side of Hitchcock that most influenced his work. By treating his own fears through the characters of his films, Hitchcock constantly reminded us that *no one* was immune to petty terrors.

Despite this, Hitchcock maintained that his movies were the antithesis of his personal life, although he wouldn't drive a car for fear of reproach from policemen. His life-style was serene, highly controlled, and yet he fretted and worried like the rest of us and did not always know precisely what he hoped to achieve. Nevertheless, following his instincts, he gave his public films that were wonderfully entertaining and reminded them that, like himself, things were not always what they seemed.

One of the most intriguing elements in the Hitchcock universe was his puckish sense of humor. He was a typical Englishman, with a finely honed sense of wit—dry as a kipper and twice as salty. He adored practical jokes and the barbed riposte that resonated with the ring of truth. Also, he was unshakably opinionated. He once told a young, struggling actor, "I can't understand why you are all atwitter. There's nothing depending upon your performances except your whole career."

His reputation for sarcastic wit was matched with his studied habit of never raising his voice or arguing on the set. Of course, there were some notable exceptions which will be discussed later. It should be remembered that everyone has his or her limits of patience, even Hitchcock, but the imposing Hitchcock manner proved a successful device in dominating most situations and exemplified his desire to remain detached from the grubbiness of life. "My aim," he once declared, "is quiet dignity." What better living for a man of "quiet dignity" than making movies where he could examine the seamier sides of life without actually becoming involved in them.

His sense of humor and his natural public-relations instincts led to the most visible of all the Hitchcock devices—his cameo appearances in his films. Originally conceived out of necessity (he couldn't afford another film extra), the Hitchcock cameos became legendary. Soon he realized how eager people were to see him, and he would try to appear as early as possible so as not to distract attention from the story line. He enjoyed making his guest appearance as unlikely as possible, as will be seen later in this book's section on the cameos.

Hitchcock was a keen observer not only of others, but of himself. He was well aware of his peculiarities and fears and, in the case of his cameos, his size. He was, he readily admitted, always fat. From pleasantly plump as a child, to near 290 pounds at his heaviest, he was a steady dieter but an unsuccessful one. He stated the case more plainly, "A New York doctor once told me that I'm an adrenal type," he quipped. "That apparently means that I'm all body and only vestigial legs. But since I'm neither a mile runner nor a dancer, and my present interest in my body is

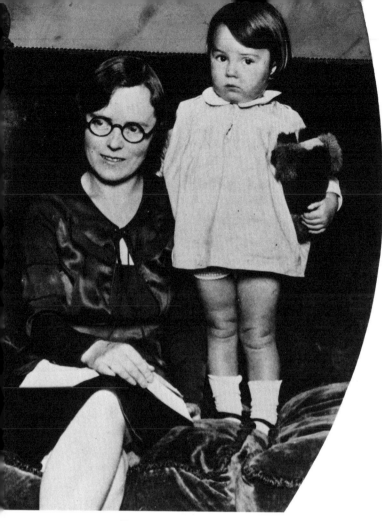

Petite and shy, Alma Reville was a film editor when Hitchcock was an assistant director. Their marriage consolidated a formidable team, joined later by daughter, Patricia, pictured here.
(The British Film Institute/National Film Archive/ Stills Library)

almost altogether from the waist up, that didn't bother me much."

There were two women who could claim to completely absorb the master of suspense—his wife, Alma, and his daughter, Patricia. Mrs. Hitchcock was the former Alma Reville, a film editor in England when Hitchcock was a title-card designer. After a long friendship and a most unromantic proposal, the Hitchcocks began their most important career together—their marriage. This union was especially unusual to bed-hopping Hollywood. Normally, he was home by five, and Alma fixed

his meals herself. Invariably, on the first day of shooting, Alma was in a chair at the director's side.

Patricia, their only child, was born on July 7, 1928, and enjoyed the attention of a proud and doting father— a response by Hitchcock to his own often lonely childhood. She later became interested in acting and was seen in several of her father's works but decided, as Hitchcock put it, ". . . that being a mother of sticky-fingered children required all her creative attention."

There are few directors who would not be satisfied with making fifty-three feature movies, most successful and several considered the finest ever produced. But the Hitchcock legacy does not stop there. On October 2, 1955, CBS began showing *Alfred Hitchcock Presents,* one of the most popular television series ever broadcast. The remarkable outpouring of 365 shows over a period of seven years did more to popularize Hitchcock than any other thing in his career—not because he

The Hitchcocks lived quietly in the same house in Bel Air for many years after moving to America.
(The Museum of Modern Art/Film Stills Archive)

personally directed the shows (although he did direct seventeen of them), but because he introduced them as the master of ceremonies. And what introductions they were!

The show always opened with the now infamous "Funeral March of a Marionette" and the silhouetted image of "His Malevolence" stepping into his own equally famous profile sketch. Then he delivered his introduction. These brief, outrageous vignettes had Hitchcock costumed in every guise imaginable, from Queen Victoria to a man with a hatchet buried in his head. They were written by the gifted James Allardyce, and designed to abuse that great sacred cow—the sponsor. Hitchcock had a special theory about television commercials—he despised them—and he let the public know it. This brought on an epidemic of lifted eyebrows from his backers, but when their sales went up, they looked the other way. The public, needless to add, ate it up.

Alfred Hitchcock Presents spun off into the *Alfred Hitchcock Mystery Magazine* and a host of paperbacks bearing the Hitchcock image and seal of approval. All of these enterprises were run by various companies, and Hitchcock had little to do with them but endorse the checks.

During this time, several other equally lucrative financial events occurred which insured Hitchcock's fortune and made him one of the wealthiest men in Hollywood. Much of his wealth was the result of a sound business mind and the placement of trust in his one-time agent and business manager, Lew Wasserman. At one point, Wasserman converted Hitchcock's interest in the Hitchcock television series into MCA stock, which meant that when he died, Hitchcock was a large shareholder in Universal Pictures, the show's producer.

The young engineering student had yet to develop his famous profile. He was absorbed by the theater and a love for American technical film magazines. (The British Film Institute/National Film Archive/Still Library)

He was a shrewd businessman, but never seemed to be enamored of his riches, preferring to let them pile up for posterity and for his family. He enjoyed rented limousines, fine wines and cigars, and he was an ardent collector of the work of the renowned abstractionist, Paul Klee. His passion, though, was making movies. "The mooo-vies," as he said it, were his life's work. His family was his life.

It sounds rather simple, doesn't it? But this was a complex man with a vision. There is much to learn from Hitchcock in how we perceive each other and ourselves. Hitchcock was a practical man with an artistic sensitivity who could assess the human condition and, by entertaining us, make *us* perceive it too. This remarkable talent was never "a matter of carelessness."

"Not a bad guy . . . although not exactly a man to go camping with."—*David O. Selznick*

 There was something oddly prophetic about the pudgy fourteen-year-old boy, who was not academically inclined, memorizing travel maps, the stops on the Orient Express, the complete geography of New York City, and traveling every inch of the London General Omnibus Company's routes by himself. Young Alfred Hitchcock *was* this curious child who engaged in a multitude of self-created games he would play alone. John Russell Taylor, in his authorized biography, *Hitch,* delves into various theories about Hitchcock's upbringing, but most of it remains theory. Little exists in the way of background on the young Briton except his own rare reminiscences and those of his family. He had few friends—partly by circumstance, but mainly by choice. Shy, retiring, and, as he put it, "an uncommonly unattractive young man," Hitchcock seems to have started early keeping himself to himself.

He was the last of three children of William and Emma Hitchcock, born on August 13, 1899. They were a merchant family in Leytonstone, England, just outside London. William Hitchcock was a successful produce and poultry dealer, two enterprises which seem to have had little effect on Hitchcock, except that he developed a profound dislike for eggs. Some years ago he disputed this theory in an interview in the *Saturday Evening Post.* "It's true that I do regard eggs as loathsome, but my father's occupation had nothing to do with my reaction. To me, the most repulsive smell in the world is that which reeks from a hard-boiled egg."

As if to prove the point, in *To Catch a Thief,* a saucy and ruthless Jessie

He was born in Leytonstone, England, to a produce dealer. Pictured in front of the family business are his father and his brother, William. (The British Film Institute/National Film Archive/Still Library)

He and Alma led a very private but productive life. She was his partner, critic, and best friend, and was responsible for many of his early screenplays. (The British Film Institute/National Film Archive/Still Library)

Royce Landis extinguishes her cigarette right in the middle of an egg yolk; and in *Shadow of a Doubt,* a man is in the process of enjoying a fried egg when something shocking is said, and his knife stabs the yolk, releasing a flood of goo onto his plate. "To me," Hitchcock smiled, "it was much more effective than oozing blood."

Despite such developing predilections as a youngster, Hitchcock was about as unobtrusive as a child can be. His self-imposed loneliness was not the terrible, empty ordeal it can be for most people. It was an opportunity for thought and invention. Young Hitchcock seized upon his uncompanioned childhood to develop his imagination and was always occupied inventing games, drawing maps, and developing a compulsive interest in the way things worked. However, he was not entirely unaffected by his solitude. In later years, especially after his daugher was born, he cherished the idea of his wife and himself being home together as much as possible, and during Patricia's early childhood, of being as often as possible close by, within earshot.

Though Hitchcock never told much about his early years, he repeated one story often. At the age of five or six, after committing some minor foul

His weight was always a problem; even with dieting, it was an uneven battle. (Memory Shop)

deed (he couldn't recall what it was), his father sent him to the police station with a note. The constable read it and forthwith locked up the youth in a jail cell for five minutes, saying, "This is what we do to naughty boys." The effect was devastating. His father had always referred to him as "a little lamb without a spot," so it is difficult to understand why he chose such a dramatic punishment for a misdeed. Thereafter, Hitchcock was terrified of the police; he referred to this incident as the source of his profound fear of the police and authority figures.

     Another strong influence in his early years seems to have been his religion. He was raised—and he died— a devout Roman Catholic. His parents were not regular in worship, but they saw to it that their children were at every mass and confession. Much has been written by film critics theorizing the possible implications of a Catholic upbringing in an Anglican neighborhood, but again, the reasoning is mainly speculative. There are few signs of Hitchcock's religious background in his films, the most notable being the generally unsuccessful *I Confess,* with Montgomery Clift.

     If his religion had any major influence on his films, it was due mainly to his Catholic boarding school education, which began at the age of nine at Salesian College in Battersea. He was then ensconced for the next five years at St. Ignatius College, Stamford Hill. In Hitchcock's published interview with François Truffaut, he recalled one aspect of his education. "It was probably during this period with the Jesuits that a strong sense of fear developed—a moral fear—the fear of being involved in anything evil. I always tried to avoid it. Why? I was terrified of physical punishment. In those

days they used a cane of hard rubber. I believe the Jesuits still use it." The worst part of all, he admitted, was the procedure that was used to administer the penance. The felon's name would be inscribed in a register, together with the type of punishment to be inflicted, and then the student would have to wait for the sentence to be carried out.

     He was not a brilliant student, but neither was he slow. He told Truffaut, "They claim I was rather absentminded." It was not a permanent condition. Hitchcock excelled in geography, naturally enough, as he spent a great deal of time reading and memorizing railway timetables and Cook's travel folders. This rather unorthodox hobby would continue to fascinate him the rest of his life.

     In 1914 his father died, and Hitchcock left St. Ignatius to enter the School of Engineering and Navigation. He studied drafting, sharpened his ability to grasp *how* machinery worked, and furthered his interest in drawing. Part time, he enrolled in a course in sketching and drawing at London University. His skill at line drawing manifested itself in two distinct areas, the first being his own famous profile sketch. "I began to draw it years ago when I was a movie art director," he once remarked. "With one exception there's been little change to it since then. At one time I had more hair. All *three* of them were wavy." Indeed, the sketch changed frequently as the three wavy lines disappeared, and the semicircles became . . . more circular. For millions of television viewers, that distinctive profile stepping into those unforgettable lines was the prelude to another evening of "a little suspense and murder."

     The second area was Hitchcock's almost unprecedented habit of story-

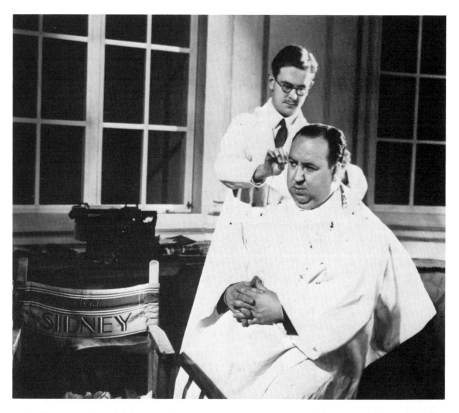

He hadn't much hair, but seemed
to think haircuts should be
recorded for posterity. Here, on
tne set of Blackmail, he expresses
another fear—scissors.
(EMI Films Limited)

As the years went by (below left),
he seemed to relax into the ritual.
(The British Film Institute/National
Film Archive/Still Library)

Finally, he discovered the secret:
a tall, beautiful blonde—
Grace Kelly dressed for the ball
scene in To Catch a Thief.
(The British Film Institute/National
Film Archive/Still Library)

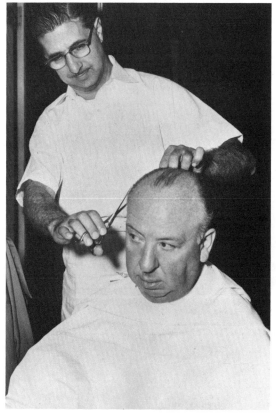

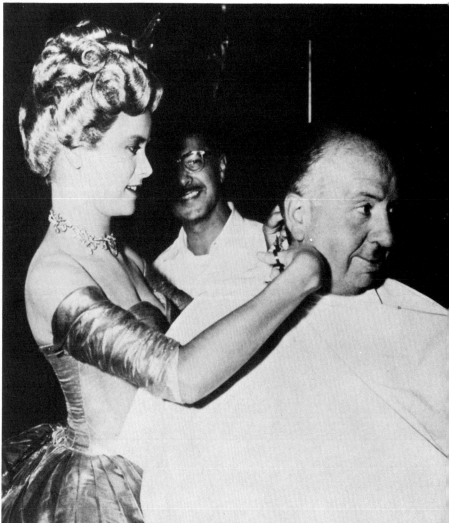

boarding his films. Storyboarding was a process used mainly by animators, who would carefully outline the key frames of their film by making sketches. Hitchcock made hundreds of sketches himself for his early films. In later years he had sketch artists perform this laborious task. He maintained that the actual shooting of a movie was quite boring to him; he already knew what the finished film was going to look like!

The storyboard concept of making a film came about for several reasons. It reflected Hitchcock's background in the early silents, when there was never much money available and it was essential to shoot only as much film stock as necessary. By outlining the entire film in advance on the storyboard, he seldom wasted footage. As a result, Hitchcock often brought his pictures in under budget. Besides frugality, his careful and prerealized vision of what he was doing accounts for the orchestrated quality of his movies. He knew what he wanted, so why shoot it another way? Moreover, Hitchcock's stingy footage afforded no opportunity for studios to rearrange his shots and scenes.

After his engineering training, Hitchcock became a technical clerk at the W. T. Henley Telegraph Company, a local electric cable manufacturer. He moved quickly to estimating clerk and, after showing a little inconsistency in getting his estimates completed on time, he was moved to the advertising department. John Russell Taylor's biography, *Hitch,* notes that Henley's was becoming aware of a distinct quality in Hitchcock that prompted them to advance him into a more creative area—his extreme self-confidence. The shyness in his personality had disappeared by the time he reached adulthood.

What emerged was a watchful, patient young man, slightly extroverted, who was willing to tackle anything.

Taylor describes one of Hitchcock's first attempts at the psychological manipulation of an audience. He was asked by Henley's to create an advertisement for a specially designed lead-covered wire for use in churches and historic buildings, where it would be invisible against the old stonework. What he came up with was a brochure that was upright and coffin-shaped, with an altar frontal at the bottom holding two large brass candlesticks and, in heavy Gothic letters at the top of the page, the words *Church Lighting.* Since the whole point of the product was its invisibility, there was no mention of electricity, and the rather macabre design created a sensation that was not related to the product but certainly held readers' interest. The ad manager's response was "Very clever. But don't tell him I said so!"

It was during this time that his artistic interests were becoming evident. Already he was an enthusiastic theatergoer and movie fan. He spent many hours watching stage plays and the silent films of Chaplin and Griffith. From the age of sixteen he had been reading film journals and technical magazines. His interest in filmmaking was not just a teenager's fantasy, but a deeper and developing interest in a possible field of endeavor.

In 1919 he read that the Hollywood film company Famous Players-Lasky, the predecessor to Paramount Pictures, was building a studio in Islington, and Hitchcock decided to get into "the mooo-vies." How to accomplish this was a problem for the twenty-year old, who had no practical experience at moviemaking. His solution was simple. He found out what the studio's first

This screaming face is the opening shot of Hitchcock's great silent film, The Lodger. *The audience's imagination provided the sound.* (The Rank Organization Limited)

picture would be, and then he went out and purchased a copy of the novel it was based on—Marie Corelli's *The Sorrows of Satan.* Capitalizing on his sketching abilities, he designed several title cards (the cards that carried the dialogue and, usually, an illustration) and trotted over to the new studio to present them. However, when he got there they'd changed their plans. No matter. He made a new set for the new picture, returned, and the studio gave him a part-time job as a title-card designer.

In a short time Hitchcock was on the full-time staff. During the next three years he designed cards for all eleven films that Famous Players-Lasky made in Great Britain. In the meantime, Hitchcock was committing to memory every detail of the techniques of filmmaking he could discover. He learned that it was quite easy to manipulate an audience by arranging and cutting a set of film images. If a film was shot as a drama but the acting was awful, one could re-edit, insert new titles, and come up with a dandy comedy. He was especially conscious of the power of the director to take various neutral elements (actors, scenery, dialogue, and plot) and arrange them to fit his particular vision of a story. It was a most important lesson, one he never forgot.

At the time, Hitchcock hadn't the slightest interest in becoming a director; he was more concerned about merely being involved in the film-making process. A specific position was not on his mind. Then he was asked to direct one of Famous Players-Lasky's silent shorts. It was called *Number Thirteen* and was never finished. It doesn't exist today, a stroke of luck as far as Hitchcock was concerned. Soon thereafter, another chance came in 1923, when the director of a one-reel comedy called *Always Tell Your Wife* became sick and Hitchcock, as his assistant, filled in. Just as he was starting to enjoy this newfound challenge, Famous Players-Lasky closed shop and returned to Hollywood.

The Islington Studio reopened in British hands and became Balcon-Saville-Freedman. One of the first people they hired was the young assistant director they had noticed for his previous work. Balcon-Saville owned a property called *Woman to Woman* as their first venture. They found their new employee ready to tackle not only his assistant directing task, but the scripting and art direction as well. During the next thirty weeks, he assisted with the making of six films, taking on chores he wasn't asked to do and generally making himself invaluable.

His new bosses did something more than give Hitchcock a fresh and exciting responsibility—they also hired a film editor named Alma Reville. She came from a family involved in film, her father being an employee of the Twickenham Studio. She had started work at sixteen and had edited several major films for that studio. Until he was made an assistant director, Hitchcock remained aloof, and then his tune

changed. In the Taylor biography of Hitchcock, Alma sums up the exact reason for Hitchcock's reticence, "Since it was unthinkable for a British male to admit that a woman has a job more important that his, 'Hitch' waited to speak to me until he had a higher position."

At the time he met Alma, "Hitch" (as he was called by his friends) had never dated except to take his sister to a dance once. Also, like many proper young lads his age, he knew nothing about women. In short, he must have been quite smitten even to have dared talk to this cool young woman with the impressive film credits.

Michael Balcon, one of the producers, had been observing the energetic young man and decided that there was no reason to keep him on as an assistant. So he assigned him to his first feature-length picture, *The Pleasure Garden.*

Most of Hitchcock's problems with the picture revolved around money—there wasn't enough of it. This situation was compounded when he was robbed of all his cash while on location. Unstymied, he called his producer for an advance and proceeded to film a scene at the beach; one in which a man drowns a woman while pretending to rescue her. When all was in readiness, he discovered the camera-man and the actress in deep discussion. She refused to go into the water. Why not, he asked. It's that time of the month. What time of the month, he inquired. Whereupon he was given a detailed lesson in female physiology by the cameraman. His reaction was sublime! Why the hell didn't she tell him before he spent all that money to bring her from Munich to San Remo? She was immediately shipped back.

He found a replacement, but she was a few pounds heftier. Every time

16

The Lodger, based on the Jack the Ripper story, starred Ivor Novello as the suspected killer, seen here taking a room in a boarding house.
(The Rank Organization Limited)

his leading man, Miles Mander, had to drag the "body" out of the ocean, he dropped her. Just as he managed to "beach the whale," a little old lady gathering shells walked up to the camera, stared in the lens, and the film crew had to start over again!

The film was completed with much difficulty and became a mild success, whereupon Hitchcock immediately filmed his second picture, *The Mountain Eagle.* No trace remains of this film, "which is no great loss," according to Hitchcock. His only comment about that film is found in François Truffaut's book. "The producers were always trying to break into the American market, so they sent me Nita Naldi, the successor to Theda Bara for the part of the village schoolmistress. She had fingernails out to there. Ridiculous!"

The fate of his first two silents faded with the making of his third film, *The Lodger,* which is still shown and considered among one of the most innovative silent movies ever made. The script, based on the book of the same name by Mrs. Belloc Lowndes, starred then-current screen heartthrob, Ivor Novello. The story line was based on the Jack the Ripper murders, where a man is mistaken for the demented doctor. It is the first true Hitchcock film, with many of his soon-to-be-famous story themes, and containing the type of visual suspense that was to become his hallmark.

With Alma as his assistant director (she had acted in the same capacity for his previous two films), he brought a wealth of imagination to the picture. One of the more famous scenes is one in which Ivor Novello is nervously stalking the floor of his rented flat. Downstairs, the family listens and wonders about their strange boarder. By placing Novello on a sheet of one-

17

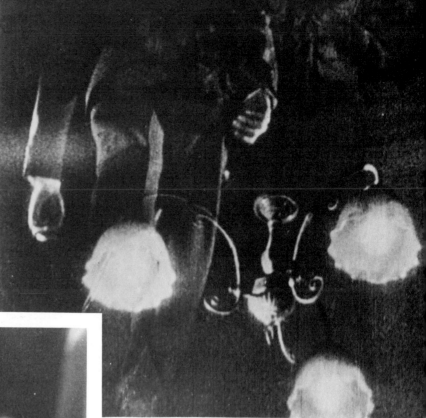

Hitchcock stretched his imagination in The Lodger *to illustrate the nervous pacing of Ivor Novello by filming him through a glass floor.* (The Rank Organization Limited)

The Lodger *ends with Novello being pursued by a mob, to be finally trapped in this crucifixion pose just before he is found innocent.* (The Rank Organization Limited)

inch-thick plate glass and shooting from underneath, Hitchcock shows the suspected man's feet treading back and forth as the family listens to his footfalls. He commented later that the same effect could have been accomplished by just showing the chandelier moving, but the critics were awed by this technical invention and hailed the film as a masterpiece.

By using fewer titles and stark, vivid screen images, Hitchcock created a tale of unnerving simplicity and suspense. It endeared Hitchcock to the critics, and not one to waste the opportunity to encourage them, he soon learned the wisdom of taking them to lunch and always returning their phone calls.

It was a glorious time for Hitchcock. He became an instant success at twenty-seven years of age. He added frosting to the cake by marrying Alma Reville on December 2, 1926, in a side chapel of Brompton Oratory. They honeymooned at the Palace Hotel in St.

Downhill, his next silent, again starred Ivor Novello. Novello had written the stage play and tried to pass as the schoolboy hero.
(The Rank Organization Limited)

Moritz, and the sentimental Hitchcock made a habit of returning with Alma, and eventually with daughter, Pat, every possible Christmas season thereafter.

Hitchcock was becoming an amusing eccentric and practical joker. At home, he was compulsive—he always cleaned and dried a washbasin after washing his hands. On the set and in public, he was a ham. He developed the curious habit of drinking large quantities of tea, and when he finished a cup, he hurled the empty cup behind him. It became a drain on the porcelain, but a calculated way to keep his crew on its toes. His practical jokes became legendary. He placed a full-size workhorse in the dressing room of his actor-friend, Sir Gerald Du Maurier. He had oversized furniture put in friends' apartments, gave strange birthday gifts (such as four-hundred smoked herring), and once served an entire dinner where all the food was blue—blue soup, blue trout, blue chicken, and blue ice cream. "It seemed such a pretty color, I couldn't understand why hardly anything we eat is blue." Of course, the elevator stories were notorious.

As he relates it, the elevator gag went on in the form of a dialogue with his companion in a loud voice: "Of course, I didn't know the gun was loaded, but when it went off it blasted a great hole in his neck. A flap of his flesh fell down, and I could see the white ligaments uncovered. Presently I felt wetness around my feet. I was standing in a pool of blood." Another scenario went this way: "You know, she married four times, and it just so happened that

she had a child by each one. Well, all four of the husbands happened to meet one day, and do you know what they said . . ." With that, they would step out of the elevator and disappear!

His next film effort, *Downhill,* starred his *Lodger* hero, Ivor Novello, but it was not as successful commercially as the latter. Indeed, he made six more silents, but none achieved the popularity of *The Lodger.* He continued to amaze his contemporaries with his technical virtuosity, even though he was developing the habit of throwing logic to the wind, which disturbed some of his more conventional-minded colleagues. One, Ivor Montagu, who had done considerable editing on *The Lodger,* would write, many years later, of his differences with Hitchcock in *Sight and Sound,* the official publication of the British Film Institute. In *The Lodger,* he had disagreed with the director over a shot of a hand switching off a light, arguing that it was not logical for the light to go off *after* the switch was thrown. However, he conceded it was a minor point.

Montagu edited *Downhill* and began preliminary work on *Easy Virtue,*

19

Easy Virtue, *showed such risqué scenes as this played in a bedroom by Isabel Jeans and Robin Irvine.* (The Rank Organization Limited)

over which he and Hitchcock locked horns. The shot in question was composed of three people in the rear seat of a taxi—a wife, a husband, and the wife's lover. In order to show the interplay of a game of "knee's-touch" between the lover and the wife, Hitchcock shot the scene from above, as if the top of the cab weren't there. Montagu was livid at this violation of reality, but he conceded to Hitchcock rather than lose his friendship. They remained friends, but did not work together again until 1934 and *The Man Who Knew Too Much.*

Easy Virtue was adapted from Noel Coward's play of the same name. Hitchcock never met Coward, although

they were almost the same age and were raised only a few miles apart. However, their paths never crossed, and the film, unfortunately, was not a great success. In fact, one of the few things Hitchcock had to say about it was that it contained the worst title he ever wrote. In the film, a famous woman is involved in a divorce case and must tell all to the court. As word spreads that this woman is baring her soul, photographers gather outside. She appears at the courthouse steps, flings open her arms, and says, "Shoot, there's nothing left to kill!"

After *Easy Virtue* came *The Ring,* which was a critical but not a commercial success. It starred Carl Brisson, a popular actor of the day, but didn't catch on at the box office. Next, *The Farmer's Wife,* which was most memorable to Hitchcock for the fact that the cameraman got sick and he had to handle

The Ring starred Carl Brisson as a prizefighter who is in love with the same girl as his rival. (EMI Films Limited)

The Farmer's Wife *was a funny and fairly well received film, and Hitchcock wound up doing much of the camera work himself when his camera operator took ill.* (EMI Films Limited)

Champagne *had no fizz, but Hitchcock did capture the human condition in this scene where Betty Balfour is interviewed for a job. Note the shoe lifting the hemline.* (EMI Films Limited)

22

the job himself. "I did what I could, but it wasn't actually very cinematic," he recalled.

His next two pictures, *Champagne* and *The Manxman,* are two films he ignored when discussing his work. Certainly *Champagne* was pretty much of a bomb, but *The Manxman* was a serious picture featuring some striking photography by Jack Cox. Set on the Isle of Man, it was actually shot on the Cornish coast. Hitchcock had only this to say about it: "The only point of interest about that movie is that it was my last silent one."

Soon, sound would appear in an initially ignored film called *The Jazz Singer.* For Hitchcock, as for many others, it would mark the end of an era. At this time, Alma gave birth to their daughter, Patricia; besides adding to his family, Hitchcock was beginning to develop a style and an attitude toward his work. It was clear he was most successful at suspense dramas, and he enjoyed creating tension in an audience out of ordinary surroundings. In an interview in the *Saturday Evening Post* in 1956 he explained this further. "Melodrama is the most highly colored form of storytelling. Its villains and heroes are usually played heavy-handedly and bumble-footedly. I approach it somewhat differently. I've never gone for the creaking door type of suspense. To me, murder by a babbling brook drenched in sunshine is more interesting than murder in a dark and noisome alley littered with dead cats and offal.

"It has been said of me that if I made *Cinderella,* the audience would start looking for a body in the pumpkin coach. That's true. If an audience sees one of my productions with no spine-tingling they're disappointed."

The Manxman *was Hitchcock's last silent film. It was not a film he liked, although the photography was striking, as evidenced in this shot of Malcolm Keen framed in outcroppings on the Cornish coast.* (EMI Films Limited)

23

"Some films are slices of life. Mine are slices of cake."
—*Alfred Hitchcock*

Hitchcock had developed a number of effective ideas about how to make a suspenseful movie. Time and again he would refer to the "MacGuffin." The phrase itself is attributed to Angus MacPhail, who frequently did scenario editing for Hitchcock. Here is the anecdote he referred to:

Two men are traveling on a train to Scotland. On the luggage rack is a large bundle.

"What is that package?" asked one of the men.

"Oh, that's a MacGuffin," replied his friend.

"What's a MacGuffin?"

"It's a device for trapping lions in the Scottish Highlands."

"But there aren't any lions in the Scottish Highlands!"

"Well, then, I guess that's not a MacGuffin."

The "MacGuffin" was to become that part of a Hitchcock plot that served to keep it moving—whether it was secret documents, a spy ring, or uranium ore, the "MacGuffin" is what the characters in the movie were trying to find out about. Most importantly, Hitchcock wanted to show what happened *to people* when they became involved in shenanigans such as murder and espionage while, at the same time, he strove not to focus an entire film on the "MacGuffin" itself. This was usually accomplished by establishing early on who the villain was, or who had the bomb, which furnishes the key to his unerring ability to keep audiences on the edge of their seats with suspense. It doesn't matter if the audience knows *what* the secret is as long as they know which of the characters know and which do not.

On many occasions he elaborated on this theory by contrasting the mechanics of two hypothetical scenes. In the first such scene, four men enter a room to play poker. Suddenly, a bomb goes off and blows everyone to smithereens; for an instant, the audience is stunned. This technique he characterized as surprise. Then, he would take the same scene and before the men enter, show a man placing a bomb under the poker table. As the men sit, joke, and smoke their cigars, the suspense builds until, just as the game is about to break up and the hands on the wired clock are about to close, someone suggests another hand of poker! This was *suspense.* "Suspense," he said, "as opposed to mystery, is giving information to an audience in order to make them worry. Whereas mystery is merely withholding information."

Occasionally, Hitchcock would move away from his theories on suspense to delve into mysteries, period pieces, and comedies. Hitchcock's inability to be as successful in these forms probably gave him more insight into what he did best. Through their very weaknesses, such films as *Murder, Jamaica Inn,* and *Mr. and Mrs. Smith* helped him to define his real abilities.

In 1929 he made his first sound film, *Blackmail.* Anny Ondra, a German actress, was featured—the first of the cool, blonde women that would be so much a part of his future films. The only problem with Miss Ondra was that when it was decided to make *Blackmail* a sound film (originally slated as a silent), it was too late to recast with an English-speaking actress. Dubbing hadn't been invented; so Hitchcock had English actress Joan Barry stand offscreen and recite the dialogue while Miss Ondra mouthed the words.

Cyril Ritchard is about to rape Anny Ondra but she will kill him. Hitchcock gave his villain a melodramatic mustache by having the actor stand in the shadows cast by a chandelier. (EMI Films Limited)

The technique proved surprisingly effective.

Another point of interest in this film was his extensive use of a trick shot called the Shuftan process, variations of which are still used today. The Shuftan process (developed by German cinematographer Eugene Shuftan, notably in Fritz Lang's *Metropolis*) involved the marriage of a painted or photographed partial set and, with mirrors, a real piece of scenery. In this way, Hitchcock was able to create a chase scene through the British Museum staged on a few studio set pieces.

It is in *Blackmail* that Hitchcock makes his first cameo appearance. He had appeared earlier in a crowd scene in *The Lodger,* as well as in another scene where he sat at a desk with his back to the camera. Both cameos were so brief in duration as to be almost unrecognizable. However, in *Blackmail,* Hitchcock creates a genuine character, establishing a droll element audiences looked forward to in future movies. (A full list of his cameos can be found in Chapter Eleven).

Meantime, musical films were enjoying immense popularity, and Hitchcock was called upon to film a story entitled *Elstree Calling.* To quote the director, the film was "of no interest whatsoever." It was dreadful, and Hitchcock was beginning to recognize that his abilities did not lie in the same direction as Busby Berkeley. He followed this futile attempt at musical movie-making with a film he never thought much of, but one with which the critics were impressed. The film version of Sean O'Casey's *Juno and the Paycock* was an exercise in transferring a stage play to the screen. However, *Murder,* his next picture, was more to his liking. One of the few whodunits Hitchcock made, it had a fair number of imaginative twists and turns, and Herbert Marshall, appearing in his first "talkie," proved perfect for the new medium.

27

In this shot, from Blackmail, *Anny Ondra reaches for the knife to kill the man who is attacking her.* (EMI Films Limited)

Later, Anny Ondra will try to pick up a knife to slice some bread while a neighbor keeps chanting the word knife. *It even looks like the same knife.* (EMI Films Limited)

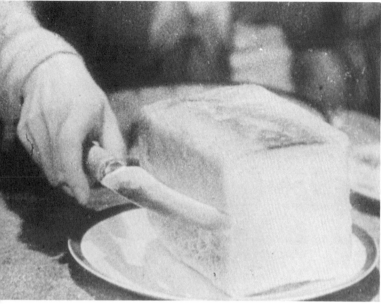

In Blackmail, *Anny Ondra is rescued by John Longden in Hitchcock's first "talkie"—his first blonde heroine.* (EMI Films Limited)

*Hitchcock had his share of failures.
Helen Burnell starred in this ill-fated musical
called* Elstree Calling.
(The British Film Institute/National Film
Archive/Still Library)

*Alma and Hitchcock worked
together on this screen adaptation of
Sean O'Casey's* Juno and the Paycock.
(The Museum of Modern Art/Film Stills Archive)

Murder brought Herbert Marshall into films.
In it, Hitchcock wanted him to be intimidatingly
rich, so he had extra padding placed
under the bearskin rug to give it luxurious depth.
(EMI Films Limited)

Hitchcock thought jail a terrifying place. In *Murder*,
with Nora Baring and Herbert Marshall, he
made it appear to be just that. (EMI Films Limited)

The Skin Game *was
another attempt at
transferring a stage play
to the screen. It starred
Edmund Gwenn,
C. V. France, and Helen
Haye.* (EMI Films Limited)

Rich and Strange *was a Hitchcock favorite.*
It starred Joan Barry and Harry Kendall as a middle-
class couple who suddenly get rich and take
an adventurous world cruise. (EMI Films Limited)

Hitchcock experimented with two techniques in *Murder.* One scene had Marshall shaving while listening to the radio. Since sound had to be recorded at the same instant as the picture, it was necessary to place a thirty-piece orchestra behind the set. They performed the prelude from *Tristan,* thus combining natural sounds with music under. He also had his actors improvise some dialogue, but none of the actors, especially Marshall, had any experience at improvisation, and Hitchcock was not well versed enough to help them. Afterward, he stuck to his preplanned style of direction.

Unfortunately, *Murder* was not as popular a movie as it could have been. Hitchcock was working outside his emerging theory; there was no "MacGuffin" in this straight whodunit; so, though there was surprise, there was little suspense.

Returning to the task of filming a stage play, he was assigned John Galsworthy's *The Skin Game.* Once again, the critics were kind but not effusive. *Rich and Strange* followed in 1931 and, as Hitchcock put it, "It had lots of ideas." The story premise was not typical Hitchcock. A young couple wins a bundle of money and takes a trip around the world. Alma was writing the screenplay (as she did for many of his pictures), so they decided to do some research on their own before starting the film. The Hitchcocks visited Paris to view the Folies Bergère, just as the couple in the movie would do. During intermission, Hitchcock asked a young man where they could watch some belly dancing, as he was planning on having his *nouveau riche* characters

31

At the end of Rich and Strange, *they are rescued from their sinking ship by a Chinese junk. In this scene, they have been given food, only to notice the ship's cat is missing.* (EMI Films Limited)

become dizzy watching a belly dancer's navel. The young man put them in a cab. "It's in the annex," he explained. When the cab arrived at its destination, Hitchcock turned to his wife and said, "I'll bet he's sent us to a brothel."

Inside, the girls presented themselves and offered champagne. The madam asked Hitchcock which young girl he wanted and inquired what could they do for his lady friend. That was enough research for the two innocents. They left immediately. Later, Hitchcock pointed out that they were behaving exactly like the couple in the planned film—naively!

For his stars he used Henry Kendall and Joan Barry, the girl who dubbed Anny Ondra's voice in *Blackmail.* The film couple run into a zoo of characters and wind up, after a shipwreck, on a Chinese junk. They return home, much wiser but still arguing with each other. It is a bizarre and interesting film, still being shown, but an unqualified failure at the box office at the time. Nonetheless, its commercial failure never troubled Hitchcock; he simply liked it.

Number Seventeen was an assigned picture and another detective story; Hitchcock wasn't particularly enthused about making it. It was a confusing and silly tale, but it did have a nifty chase at the climax between a train and a truck, achieved with miniatures. He followed this with the biggest turkey of his career—*Waltzes from Vienna.* As he told François Truffaut, "It was a musical without music, made very cheaply. In fact, at this time my reputation wasn't very good anyway, but luckily I was unaware of this."

Number Seventeen was an unsuccessful whodunit that starred Anne Grey and John Stuart.
(EMI Films Limited)

One of Hitchcock's weakest efforts was his musical without music, titled Waltzes From Vienna. *Edmund Gwenn appears in this scene.* (The British Film Institute/National Film Archive/Still Library)

The Man Who Knew Too Much *put Hitchcock back on the track. It was Peter Lorre's second movie and he portrayed a perfect Hitchcock villain; he is seen here standing between Frank Vosper and Leslie Banks.* (The Rank Organization Limited)

Now a chance came to redeem himself and apply those various techniques with which he had been tinkering. *The Man Who Knew Too Much* was a compact, fast-paced movie eighty-four minutes long that incorporated the best of the Hitchcock repertory of ideas. His "cool blonde" (Edna Best) is vacationing with her husband (Leslie Banks) and daughter (Nova Pilbeam). The "MacGuffin" (an assassination attempt which the parents learn about accidentally) causes the killers to kidnap the daughter to insure the parents' silence. The movie revolves around the rescue of the daughter.

Again, the Shuftan process is used at the end of the film in a sequence in a packed audience at Albert Music Hall. The scene was actually shot in Lime Grove Studio, with most of the audience consisting of a painting by Fortunino Matania reflected by mirrors into the camera lens. In a stroke of casting genius, Hitchcock employed a young German refugee, Peter Lorre, as the villain. Lorre had impressed him with his performance in Fritz Lang's *M.*

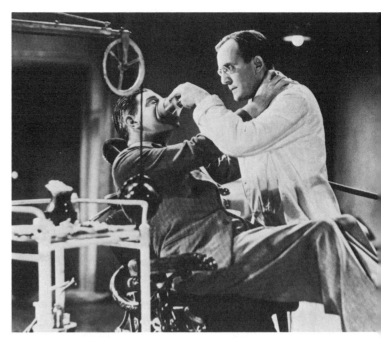

Hitchcock found terror in everyday places, such as the dentist's office in The Man Who Knew Too Much. *(The Rank Organization Limited)*

Hitchcock created a stir among the British with this scene from The Man Who Knew Too Much. *British critics didn't think it proper to show the police carrying guns.* (The Rank Organization Limited)

The 39 Steps, *now a Hitchcock classic, starred Madeleine Carroll and Robert Donat. The fast-paced story is still an exciting, often imitated narrative.* (The Rank Organization Limited)

On the heels of the critical and financial success of *The Man Who Knew Too Much,* Hitchcock made the equally notable *The 39 Steps,* with Robert Donat and Madeleine Carroll. This is a film that is truly timeless and full of odd twists. It is the forerunner of a favorite Hitchcock scenario: an innocent forced to clear himself of a crime he did not commit. He liked Madeleine Carroll as his blonde heroine in the film, but he thought her nose had been raised a little too high by Hollywood and delighted in inventing a host of slightly degrading stunts for her to do, such as being dragged through one muddy stream after another. The movie was so popular it has been remade twice by others, but neither film has been close to Hitchcock's black and white version in excitement and suspense. (In 1960, director Ralph Thomas featured Kenneth More and Taina Elg in a splashy color version of the thriller, and twenty years later, Don Sharp tried again with Robert Powell and Karen Dotrice the stars.)

In similar fashion, over the years many directors have tried to imitate Hitchcock for one reason or another. Notably, Mel Brooks made a spoof of *Vertigo* and other Hitchcock films called *High Anxiety,* and Brian DePalma directed movies such as *Obsession* and *Dressed to Kill.* Both employ a variety of Hitchcockian techniques and camera movements. DePalma has defended his homage, remarking that Hitchcock "created a vocabulary" and that he was trying to learn to speak that tongue.

Hitchcock never seemed flattered by his imitators. Indeed, it is speculated that his adverse reaction to DePalma's "tribute" was the reason five Hitchcock films have been out of circulation for some time. These pictures—*Rope, Vertigo, The Man Who Knew Too Much* (the 1956 remake), *Rear Window,* and *The Trouble With Harry*—were owned outright by Hitchcock and have been off the market for years. (*Psycho,* also owned by Hitchcock, was later sold to Universal.)

In this regard, it is unusual for studio-financed films to revert to the director or an actor. The only people known to have achieved this are Hitchcock, Otto Preminger, and Cary Grant. Herman Citron, Hitchcock's agent at the time of his death and the man in charge of the estate's film affairs, was quoted as saying, "I think the films will be back in circulation soon." It will be a great gift to the public to have them back.

In The 39 Steps, *Hitchcock developed outrageous stunts for Madeleine Carroll to perform, such as having her handcuffed to Robert Donat and dragged through one muddy stream after another. There were other kinds of comic relief as well.* (The Rank Organization Limited)

*Hitchcock liked villains to be appealing,
thus Robert Young was the perfect
choice for* Secret Agent, *with
Madeleine Carroll.*
(The Rank Organization Limited)

In Secret Agent, *Peter Lorre plays
a sleazy good guy and friend to
John Gielgud. In this scene he tries to
join Lilli Palmer for breakfast in bed.*
(The Rank Organization Limited)

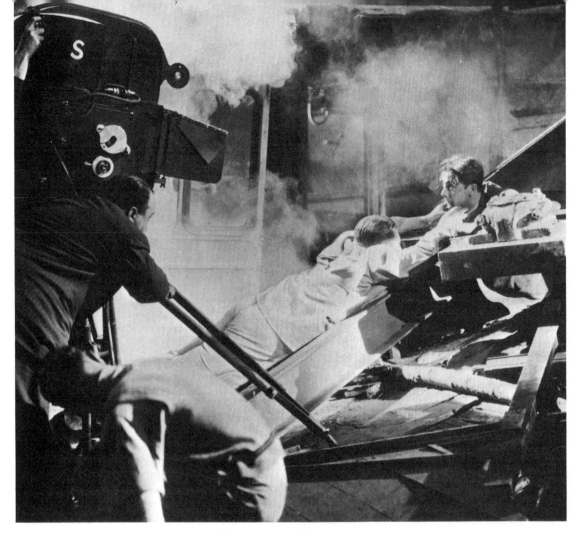

*Here, Hitchcock is seen directing Robert Young's
death in a train crash from* Secret Agent.
(The Rank Organization Limited)

His next picture, made in 1936,
starred John Gielgud, Robert Young,
Madeleine Carroll, and Peter Lorre.
The Secret Agent was based on Somerset
Maugham's book. Gielgud was not all
that thrilled about appearing in the
picture, but he was Hitchcock's choice
and, as it turned out, not a good one. He
tended to be a little dull—but so was the
story, which involved a secret agent
sent to kill a man in Switzerland. He
assassinates the wrong man and is led—
unwillingly, by fate—to watch the right
one die. If Hitchcock wasn't too sharp
about whom he selected as a hero,
he made up for it with his choice of the

villain, the charming Robert Young. He
is the first in a gallery of Hitchcock's
more interesting characters—villains
you love to hate. Time and again,
in future films, audiences will be set
against themselves by having the
"bad guy" more likable than the "good
guy." It is an approach about which
many critics have speculated (including
theories revolving about Hitchcock's
Catholicism). None have argued
that it wasn't an entertaining perspective
on villainy.

Using the same formula, he cast
Peter Lorre (looking unusually despicable)
as the hero's friend, a Mexican general
who can't keep his hands off women.
Hitchcock was quite fond of Lorre
personally, and even tolerated his
frequent absences to shoot up with
morphine.

Sabotage *is often confused with Hitchcock's later film* Saboteur. *This one starred Sylvia Sidney and Oscar Homolka. In this scene, Sidney is about to use her carving knife on Homolka.* (The Rank Organization Limited)

Hitchcock confers on the set of Sabotage *with Oscar Homolka, who portrays the villain.* (The Rank Organization Limited)

In the same year he made *Sabotage* (released in America as *A Woman Alone*), which is often confused with another of his films, *Saboteur.* The film was based on Joseph Conrad's *The Secret Agent.* It tells of an anarchist who owns a small movie house and is trying to destroy London by setting off bombs. Oscar Homolka, a brilliant character actor, played the villain. Sylvia Sidney played the wife, and John Loder, the detective hero. There are a couple of scenes in this film which are good examples of Hitchcock overreaching and Hitchcock succeeding.

After being suspected as the saboteur, Homolka gives a bomb, disguised in a film canister, to his wife's little brother to deliver, with more than enough time for him to return unharmed. Hitchcock uses his "MacGuffin" theory of suspense to the nth degree by having the boy repeatedly delayed on his journey. Then Hitchcock commits the fatal error of not getting the boy out of his predicament. The young lad takes a seat on a bus and begins playing with a cute puppy when the bomb explodes. British audiences were quite upset. Later Hitchcock thought that the boy should have been killed by Homolka himself and not in the bomb blast. However, the boy's death is necessary, in terms of story, to set up Sylvia Sidney's vengeful murder of Homolka. The scene begins as Sidney is preparing to carve a roast for her husband just after she's realized he is the cause of her brother's death. By flashing back and forth between closeups of her hand, her face, and the carving knife, Hitchcock sets up a powerful emotional sequence which ends with Homolka *letting* himself be stabbed.

Young and Innocent, in 1937, begins (like his much later 1973 movie, *Frenzy*) with a woman's body floating in a river. The innocent man theme is used to launch the story on a chase to prove that the hero (Derrick de Marney) didn't commit the crime. As his heroine, he brings back a now more mature Nova Pilbeam, the kidnapped girl used in Hitchcock's first version of *The Man Who Knew Too Much.*

Young and Innocent contains a type of shot that was to become a trademark for Hitchcock—the long crane shot without breaks. It was an effective technique he would vary and use repeatedly. In *Young and Innocent* it is saved for the end of the movie to

In Young and Innocent, *Hitchcock used a long tracking shot that moved 145 feet to within 4 inches of an actor's face. The feat required a special crane.* (The Rank Organization Limited)

reveal the true murderer. The young protagonists have found a tramp who can identify the killer, and he tells them that the man has twitching eyes. The trio winds up at a large hotel with a dance in progress, and the tramp says, "Isn't it ridiculous to try to spot a pair of twitching eyes in a crowd this size!" With that, the camera cuts to a view of the hotel lobby from above. Slowly, it moves down through the lobby, into the ballroom, across the crowd of dancers, and straight to the dance band made up in blackface, closing in on the eyes of the drummer—which suddenly twitch. This shot required a special crane and the largest sound stage on Pinewood's lot so it could move from 145 feet to within 4 inches of the actor playing the drummer.

41

The Lady Vanishes *is considered one of Hitchcock's best films. It is a bright and witty suspense movie with the improbable pair of Haughton Wayne and Basil Radford (on the right) trying to get to a cricket match despite the intrigue around them.* (The Rank Organization Limited)

Paul Lukas and the evil baroness (played by Lary Clare) shoot it out with the good guys in the finale of The Lady Vanishes. *(The Rank Organization* Limited)

Michael Redgrave was featured in The Lady Vanishes, *his first film starring role, with the popular Margaret Lockwood.* (The Rank Organization Limited)

Working on a smaller scale, he shot a popular movie called *The Lady Vanishes* in 1938 on a single 90-foot set that relied heavily on transparencies and miniatures. It was an amusing picture, a prime example of Hitchcock at his most illogical. Many consider it one of his best films. In fact, James Thurber is said to have seen it thirteen times, and Orson Welles, eleven.

The Lady Vanishes is notable for its cast and characterizations as well. Michael Redgrave appears in his first starring role, with the already popular and beautiful Margaret Lockwood, and Dame May Whitty as a most unlikely (and illogical) British spy. Hitchcock created a marvelous duo of nincompoops from two esteemed actors of the day, Naunton Wayne and Basil Radford. They move blithely through the film, more concerned with getting to their cricket match than with the constant comings and goings of various dead bodies.

This picture was the fifth film in four years for Hitchcock, and, together

with the preceding four, is a prime
example of what came to be known as a
"Hitchcock movie"—light, suspenseful,
fast-paced. It was the peak of his
career in Britain. Soon he received
various offers from America, and he
decided to take them seriously. He
must have been slightly distracted. What
better reason for a movie as weak as
Jamaica Inn.

It was just not his cup of tea. It was
a whodunit *and* a period piece. Never
comfortable with period or costume
movies, he maintained that he couldn't
understand a scene or setting if he
hadn't *been* there. He wanted to know all
the details, understand his characters—
how they walked, how they dressed,
how they lived. Without such information, he was unsure of himself. In
spite of this, the movie was produced
by Erich Pommer and Charles
Laughton, as a starring vehicle for
Laughton, with Hitchcock directing. Set
in the eighteenth century, it even
features a cameo of Hitchcock in
costume. Hitchcock and Laughton were
friends, but not of the same creative
cast when it came to film. Laughton's
constant preoccupation with the proper
motivation drove Hitchcock to dis-
traction. Hitchcock is later quoted as
saying, "He (Laughton) wasn't really a
professional film man."

Despite its inevitable trouncing
from the critics, *Jamaica Inn* was a
financial success and brought Hitchcock
to the end of his British contract.
Soon he was lured to Hollywood by the
persuasive, loquacious David O.
Selznick. He left England intending his
trip to America to be only a visit.

Jamaica Inn *was Hitchcock's last British picture,
produced by its star, Charles Laughton. It was a
critical flop, but it did make money at the box office.*
(The Museum of Modern Art/Film Stills Archive)

"I wasn't in the least interested in Hollywood as a place. The only thing I cared about was to get into a studio to work."

—Hitchcock to Truffaut

"When David Selznick invited me to the United States to do *Rebecca,* we brought with us our little girl Patricia, a maid, cook, a cocker spaniel and a Sealyham dog. We had indifferent luck with the group: the maid got homesick and returned to England; the cook left us to become a chiropractor; and it was only through clever ruses that we persuaded the dogs to stay on." This was Hitchcock's accounting of his first experiences in Hollywood as told to the *Saturday Evening Post* in 1953.

David Selznick had finally, after a barrage of cables and wires over a period of a few years, persuaded Hitchcock to come to Hollywood to do four pictures for $800,000—a sizable sum in those days. The first picture he was assigned to direct was to be based on the *Titanic* story, but after he arrived in California, Selznick decided he should direct instead *Rebecca,* and Hitchcock agreed. While he was filming *The Lady Vanishes,* Hitchcock had thought of buying the rights to this popular novel by Daphne du Maurier, but he insisted at the time that it was too expensive.

Selznick was a new phenomenon to Hitchcock. Never before had he been required to deal with a producer who was as involved as Selznick was in the film. Immediately, he began to receive the ubiquitous Selznick memos. Selznick was infamous for his constant barrage of memoranda on the most trivial aspects of a production, and Hitchcock was no exception. Luckily for Hitchcock, Selznick became so involved in his other project, *Gone With the Wind,* that he virtually forgot about the filming of *Rebecca* once it was in production. Selznick's only meddling of

any consequence was in the selection of the female lead.

Selznick had garnered a good deal of publicity for *Gone With The Wind* by conducting an extended search for the actress to play Scarlett O'Hara. He decided that the same preproduction publicity could be performed for *Rebecca,* even though Hitchcock knew from the start whom he wanted. However, at Selznick's insistence Hitchcock made elaborate tests of Vivien Leigh, Joan Fontaine, Margaret Sullavan, Anita Louise, Loretta Young, and Anne Baxter. When it was announced that Joan Fontaine was to play the part of Laurence Olivier's wife in the picture, no one in the Hitchcock camp was surprised. She was his choice all along.

Rebecca had the largest budget Hitchcock had ever worked with, $950,000. It finally came in at nearly a million dollars. This must have been gratifying after the low budgets he had worked with in England, but now there was this problem with the film's producer. Even though Hitchcock and Selznick eventually became friends, and Selznick is quoted as saying that Hitchcock was the only director he ever really trusted, Hitchcock never quite understood or appreciated Selznick's unrelenting attention to detail and his surprise visits to the set.

Rebecca is a complex tale derived from a popular novel; so Selznick insisted that the screenplay remain faithful to the book. Joan Fontaine played a timid young girl who married wealthy landowner Maxim de Winter (Laurence Olivier). It is odd but true that the girl is never called by name in the picture. After she married Olivier, she is referred to as Mrs. de Winter. The new bride is taken to Manderley, the de Winter family estate, where she is held in contempt by the housekeeper, Mrs.

Rebecca, *Hitchcock's first effort in America,*
received the Academy Award for best picture. It
starred Joan Fontaine and Laurence Olivier.
(The Museum of Modern Art/Film Stills Archive)

Danvers (Judith Anderson), who guards
the memory of the former Mrs. de Winter,
a girl named Rebecca. The movie ends
with several plot twists and the burning
of the Manderley mansion by Mrs.
Danvers, who dies in the fire.

  Rebecca was successful at the box
office and with the critics. The film
garnered the Oscar for Best Picture and
established Hitchcock as an unqualified
success in America. It was not a movie
that was typically Hitchcock—rather
a psychological drama with romantic
overtones. Also, it was very much
an English piece with an English theme
and an all-British cast, but the scope
and the scale were decidedly American.

  Hitchcock was adjusting with
remarkable rapidity to the new
environment. He still owned a house in
England, so he had the option to remain
in America or not. He and Alma rented
a house, and Pat was enjoying her
new and sunny surroundings. Then the
war broke out between Great Britain
and Germany.

  Filming had just begun on *Rebecca*
and Hitchcock, being overage for
military service, saw no reason to leave
his contract and return to England.
Unfortunately, some of his friends in
England did not agree with his
choice, and one close friend, Michael
Balcon, denounced him publicly for not
returning. In his biography, *Hitch,*
John Russell Taylor notes that Alma took
a deep dislike to these disparaging
remarks about her husband's loyalty and
consequently became adamantly

This scene is reported to have been copied in real life. Joel McCrea is unaware that the photographer is about to assassinate *Albert Basserman in* Foreign Correspondent. (The Museum of Modern Art/Film Stills Archive)

The plane crash at the end of Foreign Correspondent *required a tank with a special track under the water so that the wing of the plane could break off and float away.* (The Museum of Modern Art/Film Stills Archive)

pro-American. She brought her mother and sister from England to live with them and took out naturalization papers five years before her husband.

In order to do his part for the war effort, Hitchcock decided to make a clearly defined anti-Nazi film. It should be remembered that at this time America was still maintaining neutrality, and the government wasn't encouraging overt declarations to the opposite effect. Hitchcock took the chance by making a film blatantly anti-Nazi in tone, *Foreign Correspondent.*

The story involved an American newspaper reporter assigned to Europe in 1939 to cover the growing threat to world peace. While in London, he becomes involved with the Nazi kid-napping of an elderly Dutch diplomat. This leads the hero to Holland, accompanied by the English girl he has fallen in love with. However, the girl's father turns out to be a Nazi agent, posing as the head of a pacifist organization, who is trying to kill the hero. They wind up on a plane to America that is shot down by Germans. The picture ends with a melodramatic but sincere speech by the hero after he and the girl are saved even as the bombs begin to fall on London.

In his interview with Hitchcock, Truffaut considered *Foreign Corres-pondent* a "B" picture compared to *Rebecca.* Hitchcock did not disagree, but blamed casting as part of the problem. Originally, he offered the lead to Gary Cooper, who declined, declaring his distaste for thrillers. His second choice was Joel McCrea, and although he was likable in the role, Hitchcock found him *too* easygoing; and Laraine Day as the girl was not as big a name as he had hoped. Nonetheless, the supporting cast was enough to make up for "star" deficiencies. Herbert Marshall

played the undercover agent for the Nazis, George Sanders moved over from *Rebecca,* and Robert Benchley provided amusing—if not entirely fitting—comic relief. Benchley is listed in the credits as well for his part of the screenwriting, as he wrote his own dialogue.

Foreign Correspondent turned out to be more expensive than *Rebecca,* with a final negative cost of one and a-half million dollars. There were several elaborate and expensive sets, including the replica of a ten-acre square in Amsterdam that could be deluged with artificially generated rain. More important, *Foreign Correspondent* contained more of the classic Hitchcock scenario elements than *Rebecca.*

It was nominated for Academy Awards for best picture and best screenplay, winning neither. However, it was a commercial success and helped reinforce Hitchcock's growing popularity with the public. Then he slipped a gear and tried his hand at a genre he never was able to master— the comedy.

The movie, *Mr. and Mrs. Smith,* starred Carole Lombard and Robert Montgomery. Though there are many comic moments in much of Hitchcock's other work, he was unable to sustain two hours of it. He admitted to Truffaut that "I really didn't know the type of people portrayed in the film. All I did was photograph the scenes as written." Unfortunately, Norman Kramer's script needed more than just good photography.

David (Robert Montgomery) and Ann (Carole Lombard) are a couple who love to pretend they hate each other. They conduct three-day fights followed by ecstatic kiss-and-make-up sessions. Then David is informed by a lawyer that their marriage is not a valid one. The

Robert Montgomery is suddenly unmarried to Carole Lombard in Mr. and Mrs. Smith. *In an effort to fall in love again, they eat at the restaurant of their youth, where even the cat won't eat the food.* (The British Film Institute/National Film Archive/Still Library)

In one of the better scenes from Mr. and Mrs. Smith, *Gene Raymond and Carole Lombard are trapped in an amusement ride.* (The British Film Institute/National Film Archive/Still Library)

Cary Grant is the husband suspected by Joan Fontaine, who won the best actress award for her portrayal of the youthful spinster-turned-wife in Suspicion. *It is Grant's first of four Hitchcock films.* (The Museum of Modern Art/Film Stills Archive)

rest of the movie involves them trying to prove to each other that they want to be married and they are willing to step up to the preacher a second time.

As always, fortune smiled again for Hitchcock when he returned to do a suspense drama, *Suspicion*. It would be his first film with one of his favorite male leads, Cary Grant. They met socially a few times, but did not become friends until they began to work together. *Suspicion* returned Joan Fontaine to Hitchcock. She would receive the Academy Award for best actress of 1941

for her portrayal of the youthful spinster, Lina MacKinlaw, in the film. Even though the movie was well cast and garnered both commercial and critical success, it was not without its problems. The studio, RKO, was constantly meddling with the finish.

As it appears today, *Suspicion* is the story of a lonely wallflower who throws herself at a handsome rake (Cary Grant) and marries him to spite her parents, who don't believe she will ever marry. After their union, he begins to show his true colors, and she begins to suspect him of trying to murder his own best friend. Then, when she discovers her name on a new life insurance policy, she believes she is going to be killed too. The pressure of her suspicion causes her to become ill, and the movie climaxes with Grant

Hitchcock used national monuments for chase scenes. In Saboteur, *the second of his antiwar films, Robert Cummings is chasing Norman Lloyd (hiding under the stairs) up the Statue of Liberty.* (Memory Shop)

bringing her a glass of presumably poisoned milk. It is a famous scene and one of Hitchcock's favorites. Grant mounts the staircase leading to her bedroom, a window casting a spiderweb-like shadow over the scene. To make the milk Grant is carrying stand out, Hitchcock had a light bulb placed inside the glass to give it a sinister glow. The milk is not poisoned, she learns that he was not trying to kill her and there is a happy ending.

However, Hitchcock had a more realistic (at least in his thinking) ending in mind. He wanted Grant to succeed

This famous shot of Cary Grant in Suspicion *is meant to convey menace. Hitchcock had a spiderweb shadow cast on the stairway and put a light in the glass of supposedly poisoned milk to make it glow in a sinister way.* (The Museum of Modern Art/Film Stills Archive)

in the murder, but with his wife giving him a letter to mail which incriminates him. He wanted the movie to end with the killer dropping the letter into a mailbox the morning after she dies. Why she would be so foolish as to drink the poisoned milk would not be explained. This version of the ending was never shot. Instead, a more complicated ending involving Grant's attempted suicide was filmed.

The basic problem was that the studio would not allow Grant to be portrayed as a villain. They were too secure with his image to allow it to be violated. So the ending with the suicide was not accepted, and the movie was cut to its present form, much to Hitchcock's consternation.

By now the war in Europe was heating up, and Hitchcock decided to do another anti-Nazi film. More strongly worded now that antifascist thinking was national, *Saboteur* starred Robert

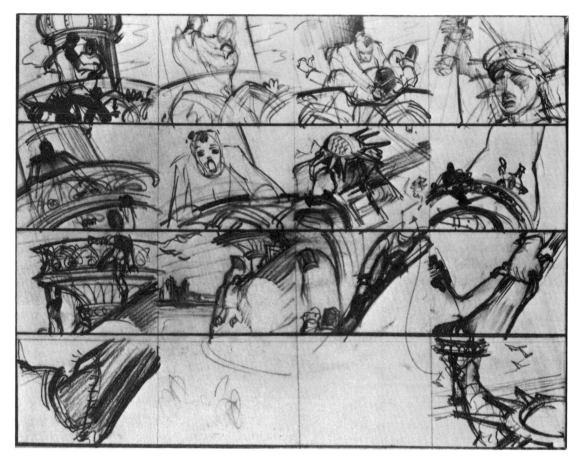

The precision of Hitchcock's movies is attributed to his use of the storyboarding technique. This is the scene from Saboteur *where Norman Lloyd falls from the Statue of Liberty, drawn by Robert Doyle.* (The Museum of Modern Art/Film Stills Archive)

Cummings and Priscilla Lane. Once again, they were not his first-choice players. He tried for Gary Cooper a second time and was again turned down. Priscilla Lane—a girl-next-door type, not the urbane sophisticate he would have preferred—was foisted on him by the studio, Universal, without his consent. But unlike *Foreign Correspondent,* the supporting cast was not a strong counterbalance. Otto Kruger was too much like everyone's image of a Nazi for Hitchcock's taste. He preferred to cast his villains against type and had asked for Harry Carey, the

western star. But Mrs. Carey would not stand for it. "After all," she told Hitchcock, "since Will Rogers' death, the youth of America have looked up to my husband!"

The screenplay was quite a combination of talents: Hitchcock did the original story and Peter Viertel, Joan Harrison, and Dorothy Parker translated it into a screenplay. Parker's contributions are strange and amusing. In one scene she has the stars in a caravan of circus performers late at night. The bearded lady has her beard in curlers and the Siamese twins fight constantly. It is a funny, compassionate scene, comparing the plight of the hero (Cummings) to the fate of the circus performers.

The hero has been framed as the man who blew up an aircraft plant. He escapes in order to gain time to clear himself, and he runs into Priscilla Lane, who tries to turn him in but then befriends him. Virtually the same story-line will be used in *North by Northwest* in later years, including the cross-country chase and the use of a national monument at the climax—in *Saboteur* it is the Statue of Liberty and in *North by Northwest,* Mount Rushmore.

It has been said that *Shadow of a Doubt,* his next picture, in 1943, is one of his favorites. In speaking to Truffaut, Hitchcock clarifies that notion by indicating that there is less for his critics to complain about in the way of illogical plot twists. Everything is plausible and not left unexplained as in many of his other films. This was due to the excellent screenplay, written by Thornton Wilder, considered one of the nation's finest writers. Hitchcock told Truffaut, "In England, I'd always had the collaboration of top stars and the finest writers, but in America things were quite different. I was turned down by many stars and writers who looked down their noses at the genre I work in." So having someone like Wilder work with him was gratifying. Unfortunately, Wilder enlisted in the psychological warfare department of the U. S. Army after finishing the screenplay and had to leave Hollywood. Hitchcock felt the script needed more humor and assigned Sally Benson to add the final touches.

The story takes place in Santa Rosa, California, and was filmed on location. Charlie Cokley (Joseph Cotten) arrives for a visit with his family, trying to avoid two detectives who are trailing him. The family—a sister, her husband, and their daughter, his adoring niece (Teresa Wright)—are happy to see him, but the niece, who is especially close to her Uncle Charlie, begins to suspect

Teresa Wright was the beautiful niece of Joseph Cotten in Shadow of a Doubt, *filmed entirely on location in Santa Rosa, California.* (Memory Shop)

that he may be the man accused of killing widows for their money. The niece falls in love with one of the detectives and becomes convinced of her uncle's guilt. Then, another suspect in a different state is apprehended and the investigation terminated. However, Uncle Charlie decides his niece knows too much and tries three times to kill her. On the last attempt, he pushes her in front of a train, but fails and is instead killed himself. At his funeral, only the niece and the detective (played by MacDonald Carey) are aware of Charlie's secret.

It is a simple, clean story with no unexplained twists that might confuse an audience. It was also one of his more realistic pictures, with many of the actors being real citizens of Santa Rosa. One local girl, Edna May Wonacott, captured one of the film's larger roles as the family's younger daughter.

In an experiment he would try again, Hitchcock filmed Lifeboat *on a single set. Tallulah Bankhead starred in what many consider her finest film role; she is seen here with Walter Slezak, Mary Anderson, Canada Lee, and John Hodiak.* (The Museum of Modern Art/Film Stills Archive)

Hitchcock finished 1943 with one of his most memorable pictures, *Lifeboat.* He was fascinated with the possibility of filming an entire movie on a single set. Thus, *Lifeboat* would be the first, but certainly not the last, of his experimental films. *Rear Window* and *Rope* would be others, each with a different connective element of screen experimentation. *Lifeboat* was also one of the most successful of the movies starring Tallulah Bankhead, possibly her most famous role. Hitchcock cast Bankhead as "the most oblique, incongruous bit of casting I could think of. Isn't a lifeboat in the middle of the Atlantic the last place one would expect Tallulah?"

The movie opened with the only shot *not* done in the lifeboat—the ship going under. The rest of the film takes place on the lifeboat alone. Bankhead is sitting bedecked in fur and diamonds in the middle of the lifeboat. Slowly, the rest of the cast swims into view and climbs aboard. Eventually she will be joined by a left-wing crew member, a young Army nurse, a millionaire, a Negro ship steward, the ship's radio operator, an Englishwoman clutching her dead baby, and a seaman with a badly injured leg. The film, the third or Hitchcock's war-oriented films, is designed as microcosm of the larger war itself, as the U-boat which has sunk them is also caught in the explosion and its Nazi captain (Walter Slezak) comes aboard too. The survivors debate whether to throw the Nazi overboard, but he saves the boat in a storm and is given charge of the vessel. Subsequently, he tries to steer the boat toward a German supply ship, but the ruse is discovered by the injured seaman (William Bendix). He is murdered by the Nazi, who convinces the others the death was a suicide. Learning the truth, they beat the Nazi to death just as they reach the German supply ship, but it is sunk by an Allied vessel and they are rescued.

The picture received considerable criticism, since the Nazi appeared the strongest member of the survivors' group. Hitchcock explained, "We wanted to show that, at that moment, there were two world forces confronting each other, the democracies and the Nazis. And while the democracies were completely disorganized, all of the Germans were clearly headed in [a single] direction." His aim was to alert the democracies to lay their differences aside to concentrate on the enemy, who was strong because of his spirit of unity and determination.

The film was not a commercial success. One critic, Dorothy Thompson, said, "I'll give it ten days to get out of town." It was intended to make us share the experience of being adrift at sea, but it became tedious. Not only does the camera never leave the lifeboat, but there is no music score. For the actors it was a special torture, since the lifeboat was kept moving at all times, and the set (a water tank) was under constant barrage with artificial fog made from oil forced through dry ice. Today the film is popular and a staple of late-night television.

The war was in full swing by this time, and Hitchcock decided to return to England for a short visit. He was asked by the Ministry of Information to make two French-language shorts as tributes to the work of the French Resistance. *Bon Voyage* was the first such featurette, and it was during filming that he became aware of the deep division among the French Resistance fighters. He made this division the object of a second short, *Adventure Malgache,* which was not released. While in England, Hitchcock made peace with Michael Balcon, who could not question his patriotism as a result of these efforts. His salary for the two shorts was the standard ten pounds a week. Shortly thereafter, he returned to America to begin work on the screenplay to the book *The House of Doctor Edwardes,* which became *Spellbound.*

Spellbound is considered by many critics to be rather mediocre, but it did bring Ingrid Bergman and Hitchcock together, a definite plus for the future and for the film. Gregory Peck played the male lead, with both performers assigned to the project by Selznick, since they were under contract. The film's theme of psychoanalysis gave Hitchcock several opportunities to try out new technical ideas. One of these encompassed a dream sequence without the usual grammar of blurring and fading images used to connote that the character was dreaming. To achieve his effect, Hitchcock wanted two things: Salvador Dali to design the sequences, and staging in brilliant sunlight. Both ideas were meant to achieve vividness and sharpness in the dream sequence. Dali's architectural accuracy did

Hitchcock wanted the dream sequence in Spellbound, *designed by Salvador Dali, filmed out-of-doors to make it more stark, but David O. Selznick, the film's producer, felt this would be too expensive, so it was shot in a studio. Here, Dali inspects one of his backdrops.* (The British Film Institute/National Film Archive/Still Library)

part of the job, but Hitchcock was thwarted in his effort to film outside by the producers, who feared it would be too expensive. It was shot inside the studio.

The story involves a mental hospital whose new director, a Dr. Edwardes (Peck), arrives, meets Dr. Peterson (Bergman), and falls in love on the spot. She soon realizes that he is a mental patient who has assumed the real Dr. Edwardes's identity, and

suspects he has killed the doctor. It turns out the real killer is the institution's previous director, Dr. Murchison (Leo G. Carroll), who, confronted with the truth, commits suicide.

The suicide afforded Hitchcock another technical opportunity. He wanted to show Carroll pointing the gun at Bergman as she exposes his secret and then, having talked him out of shooting her, she leaves the room and he turns the gun on himself. Hitchcock tried to do this by filming Carroll holding the gun, but the perspective was distorted. The final effect was achieved by designing an oversized gun, attaching it to the camera so that it follows Bergman around the room. After she leaves, the gun swivels to point directly into the camera and fires. As a final touch, there is a tiny flash of red in the gunshot blast, the only color in this wholly black and white movie. The effect is dramatic.

Spellbound was fairly successful and it is shown frequently, even today, but not as often as his next picture (one of his most financially significant), *Notorious.* For this film, the casting was superb and exactly what Hitchcock wanted: Cary Grant, Ingrid Bergman, and Claude Rains as the villain. It was a film that had all the Hitchcock elements in place and in working order.

The fast-paced screenplay by Ben Hecht, who scripted most of *Spellbound,* tells of the daughter of a jailed Nazi agent, Alicia (Ingrid Bergman), who is convinced by an American agent, Devlin (Cary Grant), to work for the U.S. in order to redeem her wayward father. She accepts and flies to Rio with Grant, where they fall in love. Then she gets her assignment, which is to meet and seduce a prominent Nazi named Sebastian (Claude Rains). Grudgingly, she does so because she loves Grant.

Notorious is splendid Hitchcock. Cary Grant returned for his second venture with Hitchcock. (The Museum of Modern Art/Film Stills Archive)

Ingrid Bergman played the alcoholic daughter of a Nazi spy. Grant lures her into working for the CIA. (The Museum of Modern Art/Film Stills Archive)

Cary Grant discovers a wine bottle filled with uranium in Notorious. *This plot device caused worried government agents to follow Hitchcock for three months.* (The Museum of Modern Art/Film Stills Archive)

Rains asks her to marry him and, when she thinks Grant doesn't care about her, she accepts. She becomes involved in her husband's Nazi household and discovers that something vital is hidden in the wine cellar. With Grant as her accomplice, she throws a large party and they discover the secret—uranium ore in wine bottles. Rains finds her out and, acting on his mother's (Leopoldine Konstantin) advice, he begins to slowly poison her to death. Grant realizes what

is happening and is able to save her from the murder plot.

Ingrid Bergman proves to be ideal as a Hitchcock leading lady, moving from cool sophisticate to unseemly drunk with ease. Grant plays the handsome hero who is a bit of a lout. He is at once cold and indifferent, then tender and caring. Claude Rains, a perfect Hitchcock villain who once taught acting to Laurence Olivier and John Gielgud, almost makes us feel sorry for him, even when the audience knows he is poisoning his wife.

Good casting, a well-constructed plot, and a "MacGuffin" that appears to be totally unimportant make for solid Hitchcockian construction. In this case, screenwriter Ben Hecht and Hitchcock, looking around for the device to keep the plot moving, came upon the idea of having a wine bottle contain uranium particles. Hitchcock heard from a writer friend that there was a project in New Mexico that involved the use of uranium in connection with the construction of an atomic bomb. To check this out, Hitchcock and Hecht visited Dr. Millikan at Cal Tech. When they unassumingly announced the subject of their movie plot, the doctor nearly fell off his chair. For the next two hours he tried to convince them what a ridiculous notion such a thing as an atomic bomb was. It was only much later that Hitchcock discovered that his innocent inquiry had aroused the interest of the FBI, who trailed him for the next three months.

The success of *Notorious* was followed with a muddled and miscast whodunit, *The Paradine Case,* the last of the pictures Hitchcock owed David O. Selznick. It is Selznick who insisted Hitchcock film the story, and almost from the beginning, things were not as Hitchcock would have liked.

The story was confusing and hard

Claude Rains, the perfect Hitchcockian villain
you love to hate, and Leopoldine Konstantin watch
as Cary Grant escapes with a dying Ingrid Bergman.
(The Museum of Modern Art/Film Stills Archive)

Charles Laughton, playing a lecherous judge, attempts to seduce Gregory Peck's wife, Ann Todd, in The Paradine Case.
(The Museum of Modern Art/Film Stills Archive)

One interesting feature of The Paradine Case, *Hitchcock's last film for Selznick, was his setup to film the courtroom scene where three cameras ran simultaneously. Try to locate the cameras trained on Gregory Peck (in the wig), Louis Jourdan, and Charles Laughton.*
(The Museum of Modern Art/Film Stills Archive)

to follow; not at all a Hitchcockian tale. The wealthy Mrs. Paradine (Alida Valli), arrested for the murder of her blind, rich husband, contacts a lawyer (Gregory Peck) to defend her and he falls in love with her, convinced she is innocent. As her trial begins, Peck learns of Valli's affair with her late husband's groom (Louis Jourdan) and pursues him in court as the murderer. The judge (Charles Laughton) is aware of the defense attorney's interest in Valli and becomes hostile and vindictive in court. Valli resents Peck's attacks on Jourdan and is devastated when Jourdan kills himself. The trial ends with Valli's confession and her scathing attack on Peck. Defeated, he leaves the courtroom in disgrace to return to his loving wife (Ann Todd).

After Selznick convinced Hitchcock to direct the film, Hitchcock tried to conceive ways to make the most of his unwanted assignment. In casting, he tried to get Laurence Olivier and Ronald Colman for the part of the lawyer and Greta Garbo for the role of Mrs. Paradine, but he had to settle for players Selznick had under contract. Especially galling to Hitchcock was the casting of the groom (Louis Jourdan)—a part that called for a rough-hewn barnyard type who satisfied the civilized Mrs. Paradine's need to be degraded. Unfortunately, Jourdan couldn't have been more opposite to the type needed.

Hitchcock's second attempt at doing something worthwhile in the film was more successfully realized. He had always wondered how the police went about arresting an affluent woman; so the movie opened with Valli seated at her piano in her drawing room. The butler announced that two detectives wanted to see her. She spoke briefly to the police, and they informed her of her arrest. With quiet dignity, she told the butler that she would not be home for dinner.

It is a powerful beginning to an otherwise weak movie. Hitchcock continues this thematic approach as Valli is taken through each phase of arrest: search, disrobing, fingerprinting, and finally, the thud of the jail cell door closing behind her as she is incarcerated.

**"I used to envy Walt Disney
when he made only
cartoons. If he didn't like
an actor, he could
tear him up."**—*Hitchcock*

With his tenure with Selznick at an and, Hitchcock entered a new arena and began his own production company, Transatlantic Pictures. His first picture, *Rope,* was a unique film that took advantage of his newfound freedom. *Rope,* Hitchcock's first color film as well, is interesting for the way in which it was filmed. Hitchcock tells Truffaut, "I undertook *Rope* as a stunt, that's the only way I can describe it." In order to understand this, it is important to remember how a movie is *usually* made.

A movie consists of tiny bits of visual material (shots), which last from five to fifteen seconds on the screen. Normally, these bits and pieces are photographed separately. For example, in a scene between two people having a conversation, one character might be sitting at a desk, the other in a chair. First the person at the desk is filmed, and then the person in the chair. When the film is edited the two scenes are combined to appear that it is all taking place at one moment in time. With *Rope,* Hitchcock intended to do the editing while filming by *not* breaking the action to do new camera setups. He filmed continuously. The effect was much like watching a play.

The story takes place in one evening in a New York apartment and spans the actual length of time of the events. Two young homosexuals (John Dall and Farley Granger) have strangled a friend and concealed his body in a chest in the same room where they are throwing a party. The guests arrive, including the victim's parents and his fiancée, and the hosts' former college professor (James Stewart). As the evening progresses, they begin to drop hints as to what they've done.

This leads Stewart to figure out what has happened and turn the two thrill seekers over to the police.

The movie, although it appears not to have a single break, actually had ten. The reason is that a film reel holds only ten minutes of film, so there had to be subtle separations until a newly reloaded camera was moved into place. Hitchcock disguised this by having a character pass in front of the camera at the end of each reel and having the next shot focussed on the same person for continuity. Thus, the "seam" was covered.

The biggest challenge for the director and crew was the way in which the single set functioned. To enable the camera to maneuver, every stick of furniture and the set itself were fixed on silent rails or rollers. In this fashion, Hitchcock recalled the first day of shooting to Truffaut. "I was so scared that something would go wrong that I couldn't even look during the first take. Walls were being moved and lights were being raised and lowered. For eight minutes of consecutive shooting everything went smoothly. Then the camera panned as the two killers walked back to the chest and there, right in camera focus, was an electrician standing by the window! The first take was totally ruined."

Rope was a modest success, even though it cost nearly one and a half million dollars to produce. By today's standards, it doesn't appear expensive, but the technical requirements and Stewart's $300,000 salary drove up the price. So Hitchcock managed to make a slight profit on *Rope,* but went deep in the hole on his next picture, *Under Capricorn,* his last Transatlantic film. It cost two and a half million dollars and died at the box office, forcing his production company to close. Ultimately, the picture was

Rope was Hitchcock's first color film and a tremendous experiment. It was filmed entirely in one long, virtually unbroken take. The only "seams" came at the end of each ten-minute reel. Hitchcock is seen rehearsing Farley Granger. (The Museum of Modern Art/ Film Stills Archive)

Hitchcock became obsessed with the long take and used several in *Under Capricorn*. Here everything, including the actors, was on rollers so that all could be moved to make way for the camera. (Memory Shop)

In this photo, the wall has been moved back into place behind the actors, who appear to sit at a solid table in Under Capricorn. *Joseph Cotten is framed between the candles.* (Memory Shop)

repossessed by the bank that financed it.

Clearly, Hitchcock blamed himself for the problems with *Under Capricorn.* It was a period piece—a film genre he had had trouble with before (*Jamaica Inn*). When he didn't know from experience how people walked, thought, and went about their daily business, he was at a loss. A second problem was that he insisted on attempting long takes in several dialogue scenes. This produced an interesting cinematic effect, but it often captured the actors' long monologues, which became tedious. However, the biggest error was the casting. Hitchcock had become obsessed with the idea of using stars in his pictures and at that time, his leading lady from *Spellbound* and *Notorious,* Ingrid Bergman, was the biggest female star in America. *Under Capricorn* was being filmed in London, and Hitchcock could not resist the temptation of a triumphant return under his own production company banner with a major star. As he related to Truffaut, "All I

could think was, 'Here I am, Hitchcock, the onetime English director, returning to London with the biggest star of the day.'"

Unfortunately, much of the cost of the production went to finance Bergman's tremendous salary. It would be Hitchcock's third and last picture with Bergman (a record of performance with him that would be later equalled by Grace Kelly). And, there were clashes on the set. The problem, as Bergman saw it, was the long takes. During the shooting of one scene, she became totally exasperated at the constant shifting of walls, props, and people. One minute she would be talking to a person and the next that person, his chair, and the wall behind him would vanish! Finally she began screaming at the director. Hitchcock, who would not tolerate scenes of this sort, promptly left the set when her back was turned. Still, she was so distraught that she continued her tirade for some time, oblivious to his departure.

Then there were problems with the script. The story takes place in Sydney, Australia, in 1830. The governor's recently arrived nephew (Michael Wilding) meets an embittered

68

Ingrid Bergman starred with Joseph Cotten in
Under Capricorn, *her last Hitchcock film.*
These shots are from her ten-minute monologue—
a stunning scene. (The Museum of Modern Art/
Film Stills Archive)

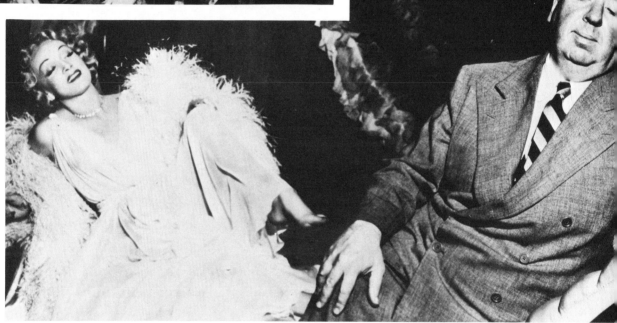

but now successful ex-convict named
Sam Flusky (Joseph Cotten) and falls
in love with his wife, Lady Henrietta
(Ingrid Bergman), a hopeless alcoholic.
Wilding attempts to help her but he is
thwarted by the housekeeper,
Milly (Margaret Leighton), who is secretly
in love with Cotten and resents Wilding's
meddling. Wilding discovers that
Bergman is being poisoned by the
housekeeper and exposes her, but
Bergman returns to her husband and
Wilding sails for England. Hitchcock had

Hume Cronyn and James Bridie as his
screenwriters; he attributed the
wordiness to Cronyn and the weak ending
to Bridie.

Stage Fright brought Hitchcock
into the fifties. Made for Warner Brothers,
it is today considered a flawed film,
but it contains a variety of interesting
moments. Hitchcock's principal interest
in Stage Fright was the plot, wherein
a struggling and naive actress is forced
to play someone else in order to reveal

the identity of a murderer. The story, by English journalist Selwyn Jepson, was reviewed as great material for a Hitchcock movie. "And I, like an idiot, believed them," Hitchcock said later.

"I did one thing in that picture I never should have done," he commented. "I put in a flashback that was a lie." As the film opens, Jonathan Cooper (Richard Todd) is recounting a harrowing experience to his friend Eve Gill (Jane Wyman). There is a flashback as he tells her that his actress-mistress (Marlene Dietrich) is framing him for the murder of her husband. He convinces Wyman to help him, and she disguises herself as a maid, gets a job with Dietrich, and, with the help of a police inspector (Michael Wilding), almost reveals Dietrich as the murderer. We learn later that the flashback was a lie told by Todd and that he is the real killer.

Jane Wyman's part called for her to assume the role of a dumpy maid, but when she saw the rushes of each day's shooting, she would try to look a little more glamorous the next day. This caused her character to become inconsistent. On the other hand, Dietrich was no problem. She played herself, got along famously with the director, and delivered a tantalizing vocal rendition of Cole Porter's "The Laziest Girl in Town."

Pat Hitchcock, his daughter, was enrolled at London's Royal Academy of Dramatic Art at the time, where part of the movie was made. So, her father used her in one of the scenes and also as Wyman's double. She was very anxious to become an actress, and her father would use her in two later films (*Strangers on a Train* and *Psycho*) and in several of his television shows.

Strangers on a Train returned Hitchcock to the solid genre of suspense where he was most confident. Briefly, the story involved Bruno Anthony (Robert Walker) and Guy Haines, a tennis star (Farley Granger), who meet on a train where Walker, a loudmouthed playboy, reveals that he is well-informed about Granger's less than private personal life: his separation from his wife (Laura Elliot) and his wish to marry Anne Morton (Ruth Roman). Walker tells Granger he hates his father and suggests that they "trade" murders. Walker will murder Granger's wife if Granger will kill Walker's father, thereby providing two crimes without motives. Walker goes ahead with his

Farley Granger and Robert Walker are Strangers on a Train, *one of Hitchcock's classic films. Walker became even more famous for his role in this picture, but died of a heart attack shortly thereafter.* (The Museum of Modern Art/ Film Stills Archive)

Robert Walker portrays a psychopathic killer who murders Granger's wife. In this scene he tells a party guest how easy it is to strangle someone, and nearly succeeds in doing it. (The Museum of Modern Art/Film Stills Archive)

part of the bargain, and soon the police suspect Granger and follow him. Later, Walker tries to frame Granger by planting Granger's cigarette lighter at the crime scene, an amusement park. In a tense race against the clock, Granger manages to chase Walker to the park and, in the ensuing fight, Walker is killed by an out-of-control carousel. As the movie ends, Walker is identified as the killer.

In this picture, Hitchcock made several good decisions which paid off with the critics and at the box office. The first was in the choice of the story—with everyone having something to feel guilty about. Even though he had problems getting a good screenplay (Raymond Chandler and he did not get along), it was an intriguing tale and gave

Hitchcock the opportunity to try many clever camera angles. Moreover, the casting was excellent for the most part. Farley Granger and Ruth Roman were contract players under assignment to Hitchcock. He was not pleased with Roman (a brunette) and only mildly satisfied with Granger (with whom he had worked on *Rope*). He would have preferred William Holden as the tennis champ, but his biggest casting coup was Robert Walker as the villain.

Up to this time, Walker had always been cast as a bland and rather comic character. Hitchcock's eye for casting against "type" made the actor a critical sensation. His brooding, psychopathic, and fey portrayal of Bruno Anthony lent *Strangers on a Train* much of its appeal. Truffaut considers Walker one of Hitchcock's three best villains, along with Joseph Cotten (*Shadow of a Doubt*) and Claude Rains (*Notorious*). Unfortunately, Walker only made one more picture, *My Son John,* in 1952. He died of a heart attack before it was released.

Montgomery Clift starred in I Confess, *a strange Hitchcock work. He played a priest accused of a murder committed by O. E. Hasse, who has confessed his crime to Clift—but Clift cannot break the seal of the confessional.*
(The Museum of Modern Art/Film Stills Archive)

In 1952 Hitchcock made *I Confess,* a picture he shot on location in Quebec, Canada. It did not enjoy the commercial success of *Strangers on a Train,* though not because it was poorly done. The problem arose with the film's point of view, which was narrow and left much of the audience unconcerned, as they did not identify with the story, which was based on a 1902 drama, *Nos Deux Consciences* (*Our Two Consciences*) by Paul Anthelme. Hitchcock had thought about doing the story for years. His chief attraction to it was the strong Catholic theme, particularly as it applied to the priest.

In the picture, a church sexton (O. E. Hasse), wearing a priest's cassock, kills a man named Vilette and then confesses his crime to Father Michael (Montgomery Clift). Unknown to the sexton, Clift is being blackmailed by Vilette over a love affair he had before becoming a priest. These two facts are enough to arouse the suspicions of the police, but Clift does not break his oath of the confessional by telling them who the murderer is. He is tried and acquitted, but is met by a furious crowd outside the courtroom. Unable to continue to see him vilified, the sexton's wife reveals the truth, and the police kill the sexton in a gun battle.

Though Hitchcock was fascinated with the idea of a priest's dilemma, the audience was not. Also, the casting

Karl Malden arrests a seemingly guilty Montgomery Clift in I Confess. *Clift studied Latin and lived in a monastery to get into character for the role.*
(The Museum Art/Film Stills Archive)

Hitchcock didn't understand method actors who thought every line should be motivated; however, he and Clift got along well. Here, Hitchcock inspects his uniform for the flashback scene.
(Memory Shop)

was not entirely consistent, for reasons beyond Hitchcock's control. His original idea for Clift's ex-lover was Anita Bjork to play the part, which called for her to be a French-Canadian. However, the Swedish actress arrived two weeks before shooting with a lover and an illegitimate baby, and Warner Brothers—the producer— objected. So Hitchcock had to settle for Anne Baxter in the role—a character for which she was not entirely suitable. But as the priest, Montgomery Clift was quite effective. His brooding and anguished character helped give the film a lot of its depth and emotional base. Nevertheless, Hitchcock did not find Clift's "method" acting technique compatible with his own approach to interpretation. Clift spent three weeks in a monastery learning the Latin mass and wearing priest's garments; later, he based his character on a certain walk.

Truffaut noted that "Clift's walk in *I Confess* is a forward motion that shapes the whole film. It also concretizes the concept of his integrity."

According to Hitchcock, the fatal flaw in the film was its lack of a sense of humor. He blamed the script for being too serious and ponderous. He contended that it was a difficult balance to strike, but that humor—or elements of it—were necessary to relieve the narrative tension and keep the viewers interested. As an example of this feat of balance he cited *Psycho.* He believed that *Psycho* was a picture with considerable humor; otherwise, he said it would have looked like a documentary.

Devastated by the weak reception for *I Confess,* Hitchcock did what he always did—he ran for cover. He felt that whenever he was making bad decisions or working with improper material, he ought to return to methods he understood best. "When you feel you're at a loss, you must go for the tried and true."

Dial M for Murder, made in 1954, would mark the start of his return to quality commercial suspense films. This trend would continue until 1964, with each film stronger than the last. *Dial M for Murder,* a popular Broadway play by Frederick Knott, fit Hitchcock's criterion for being something "tried and true." It took thirty-six days to shoot and was filmed virtually on a single, complex set. His cast was excellent and brought him together for the first time with his beloved Grace Kelly, the perfect Hitchcock female. She was the precise blend of cool, sophisticated blonde and understated sexiness he had sought after for years for his heroines. Ray Milland was marvelous as the plotting husband, and the critics

In Dial M for Murder, *while Grace Kelly talks to her husband, Ray Milland, on the phone, the assassin, played by Anthony Dawson, attempts to strangle her.* (The Museum of Modern Art/ Film Stills Archive)

joined in the praise. Robert Cummings was cast in a role better suited to his personality than that in *Saboteur,* and performed quite well.

In the story, Kelly is a wealthy woman married to a tennis player (Ray Milland) who wants to murder her for her money. He uses blackmail to persuade an old school chum (Anthony Dawson) to help him. There is a complicated plot device set up for her demise, but it is foiled when she kills her attacker instead. Milland is

disappointed at the unexpected outcome, but he behaves like a concerned husband. Eventually, a keen police inspector (John Williams) and a novelist friend (Robert Cummings) figure things out and set a trap to nab the unsuspecting husband.

This was Hitchcock's first and last venture with Naturalvision, Warner Brothers' version of the 3-D process. It was a mid-fifties fad, and most of the prints of this film were struck in the normal format since many people objected to the cumbersome, eye-straining cardboard glasses that had to be worn to view the special dimensional effects. Hitchcock did not indulge in the usual gimmicks of 3-D pictures, where things jump or are hurled at the viewing audience. His use was more subtle; it is most effective in the scene where Kelly is being strangled: as she reaches for the scissors to defend herself, her hand appears to wander outside the screen, into the audience, almost as if she is seeking help among them. Then, when the body of the would-be-killer falls, it appears to fall into the audience. Other than these instances, Hitchcock did not bother to make much of this novelty.

Hitchcock was now at the pinnacle of his career. He was able to command the actors he wanted in a screenplay and the budgets he felt he needed, and his confidence grew stronger. His next pictures—*Rear Window, To Catch A Thief, The Trouble With Harry, The Man Who Knew Too Much* (second version), and *The Wrong Man*— offer a wide and interesting variety of his talents. Even though they were not all huge commercial successes, none of them were bad films, and they do offer a mixed prelude to his succeeding four—films most closely identified with Hitchcock.

"A good film is that which absorbs the audience's attention and enables them to come out of the theater and say, 'The dinner, the baby-sitter, the price of admission—that was all worth it.'"—*Hitchcock*

Unfortunately, *Rear Window* is one of the five films Hitchcock personally owned and which he took out of circulation. It is a great loss, as it is a truly remarkable Hitchcock picture. The entire story takes place on one set, the apartment of L. B. Jeffries (James Stewart), a news photographer confined to a wheelchair with a broken leg. Bored to tears, he passes the time by spying on his neighbors with his telephoto lens. Some critics thought the premise rude and lascivious, but Hitchcock pointed out that there is a little voyeur in all of us, or the picture wouldn't have been so popular.

As Stewart watches the goings-on in the courtyard of his Greenwich Village apartment building, he becomes casually interested in one man (Raymond Burr), until he realizes that the man has murdered his wife. Stewart is unable to convince his fiancée (Grace Kelly) or a detective friend (Wendell Corey) of his dark suspicions. But eventually, Kelly does become convinced and tries to help Stewart confirm his worst fears. Ultimately, the neighbor discovers he is being watched and tries to kill Stewart, who is saved, but not without first breaking his other leg.

Of course, the use of the single set is reminiscent of *Lifeboat.* However, in this case, the set is larger and more complex, with each apartment across the courtyard comprising a mini-set in itself. The impact of *Rear Window* is not that the audience sees only one area, but that the area it observes is confined to a single point of view—Stewart's. This afforded Hitchcock the opportunity to test a theory learned while doing *Rope*: that it is more

cinematic to edit and combine scenes than to film continuously without a break. He illustrated this point to actor James Stewart by showing him a scene in which Stewart is seen looking through his 35-mm camera at a dog playing in the courtyard. First he showed Stewart a shot of him smiling and cut to a shot of the dog. Next, he took the same shot of Stewart's smile and cut to a shot of a half-naked girl exercising. The montage effect was obvious.

The entire staff and cast of *Rear Window* was a perfect mix of talent. Grace Kelly and James Stewart were making their second appearance in a Hitchcock film. It was Hitchcock's fourth movie with cinematographer Robert Burks, with whom he had worked on *Strangers on a Train.* Burks would remain Hitchcock's director of cinematography on his films until *Marnie* in 1964, with the exception of *Psycho.* He was an important asset, a close friend, and one of the factors of Hitchcock's newfound successes. Tragically, he died in 1968 in a fire in his home, which proved to be a great personal loss to Hitchcock.

Rear Window was as successful as it was inventive. "I was feeling very creative at the time, the batteries were well charged," he told Truffaut, and the "batteries" stayed up for his next film, *To Catch A Thief.* The film was his second collaboration with John Michael Hayes, the screenwriter for *Rear Window,* and their partnership was as fruitful and long-lasting as any Hitchcock ever had with a screenwriter, as Hayes would stay on board to write his next two films.

The story of *To Catch a Thief* is set on the French Riviera; it was filmed on location. It is a lush movie, and the vivid Technicolor photography

Thelma Ritter pleads with her boss, James Stewart, to stop spying on his neighbors in Rear Window. *She and Grace Kelly watch as he tries to convince them that he has witnessed a murder.* (Memory Shop)

Grace Kelly in To Catch a Thief *was the perfect Hitchcock blonde— cool outside, fiery inside.* (The Museum of Modern Art/Film Stills Archive)

would earn Burks an Academy Award. Cary Grant plays John Robie, an accomplished jewel thief and ex-member of the French Resistance during World War II. Accused of being the culprit behind a rash of jewel robberies that are upsetting the wealthy patrons of the Monacan paradise, the police aren't able to prove it. Grant is aided in his struggle to catch the real thief and clear himself by Francie Stevens (Grace Kelly), a rich, cold blonde, and her earthy mother (Jessie Royce Landis). Grant accompanies Landis and Kelly to an elaborate costume ball in order to lure the thief into the open. The plan succeeds, and Grant catches the cat burglar in a tense rooftop chase. The burglar turns out to be his own best friend's daughter.

The film is light and whimsical, filled with typical Hitchcockian twists of humor. His blonde is a vixen underneath her cool exterior, and the chase scene resembles many of his others.

His next film is one he made admittedly for himself. According to Hitchcock it is a comedy with a macabre overtone. *The Trouble With Harry* was Hitchcock's version of this sort of humor —his personal favorite. Earlier he had tried to carry it off in *Mr. and Mrs. Smith,* which failed dismally. *Harry* did not fare better at the American box office, but it did become a hit internationally, especially in France.

The story, adapted by John Michael Hayes from a Jack Trevor story,

begins on a beautiful fall day in the Vermont countryside. Suddenly, three shots ring out. A little boy (Jerry Mathers) finds a body and fetches his mother (Shirley MacLaine) to see it. The corpse is her former husband, Harry. She blames herself, having recently belted him with a bottle. Then Captain Wiles (Edmund Gwenn) thinks he is the killer, since he had been hunting rabbits in the area. For other reasons, Miss Gravely (Mildred Natwick) is sure *she* is the murderer, and a painter (John Forsythe) takes the whole affair lightly as Harry's body is repeatedly buried, exhumed, and stored in the most bizarre places. Eventually Harry is found to be the victim of a natural death, but *his* loss is everyone's gain: MacLaine falls in love with Forsythe and Gwenn with Natwick, and Harry finally gets a permanent resting place.

The Trouble With Harry *is that he's dead and no one seems to care. This macabre offbeat comedy had people literally falling over Harry's body without so much as a glance. Shirley MacLaine made her screen debut with Mildred Natwick in the film.* (The Museum of Modern Art/Film Stills Archive)

The critics were not unkind, but the film did not find an amused American public. However, it did provide a springboard for a host of new talent. This was Shirley MacLaine's first movie, and her film career caught hold after her good notices. John Forsythe had been seen on several of the Hitchcock television shows and would go on to become a major television star in his own right. Even little Jerry Mathers would go on to become the favorite of millions as the Beaver in the TV hit series, *Leave It to Beaver*.

Ironically, it is this type of humor that became the basis for Hitchcock's own successful television series. In fact, the people who would write his famous introductions on the television program were each invited to view the film to get the proper idea of what Hitchcock considered funny material.

Hitchcock has never stated publicly *why* he decided to remake *The Man Who Knew Too Much,* his next picture. One theory is that he knew James Stewart was available and wanted to use him in something he had already spent preparatory time on. When Truffaut tried to pin him down to an explanation, all he would say was, "Let's say that the first version was the work of a talented amateur and the second was made by a professional." As such, there was a considerable amount of rethinking done and several major changes made. The basic story remained the same: A family, on vacation, learns of an assassination plot. Their child is kidnapped in order to guarantee their continued silence. John Michael Hayes and Angus McPhail shared the scripting chores. They made many subtle plot changes geared to add to the excitement of the scenario.

The unmistakable Hitchcock profile was his own creation. On the set of The Trouble With Harry *he signs a sample of his work for a young Shirley MacLaine.* (The British Film Institute/ National Film Archive/Stills Library)

James Stewart and Doris Day watch an Arab get stabbed to death in a Moroccan marketplace. The dying Arab in disguise tells them a secret which results in their son's kidnapping in Hitchcock's remake of The Man Who Knew Too Much. *This film introduced Doris Day's hit "Que Sera, Sera," which won an Academy Award for best song of 1956. (Memory Shop)*

The first change was in locale; instead of Switzerland, the picture opens in Morocco, which immediately makes the atmosphere of the picture more exotic and hazardous. Stewart is joined by Doris Day, who plays a retired musical star, not a markswoman, as in the earlier version. Instead of a daughter, they now have a son (Christofer Olsen). While on vacation, they meet Mr. and Mrs. Drayton (Brenda De Banzio and Bernard Miles) and a Frenchman, Louis Bernard (Daniel Gelin), who invites them to dinner. The Frenchman cancels at the last minute, and they wind up having dinner with the Draytons. The next day they are shopping with the Draytons when an Arab is stabbed in the back in an open marketplace. He falls near Stewart and reveals his identity as the Frenchman, and whispers information about the assassination attempt to Stewart. Stewart and Day find out the Draytons are part of the plot. It is they who kidnap their son and take him to London.

In London, they go to the place where the Frenchman told them to locate Ambrose Chapel. After a false start, Stewart realizes Ambrose Chapel is a *church*, not a *person;* so Stewart goes there and discovers the Draytons. In the meantime, Day is at Albert Hall (actually filmed there) trying to locate a certain Scotland Yard detective. The assassin recognizes her and tells her to leave if she wants to see her son alive.

At the last minute, Day screams and saves the targeted diplomat's life during the concert. The diplomat takes her and Stewart to his embassy to thank them and asks her to sing one of the songs she made famous. The tune, "Que Sera, Sera," happens to be one of her missing son's favorites. He is being held in the embassy and he overhears

the song. With the aid of Mrs. Drayton, he escapes to his mother.

"Que Sera, Sera" was voted best song of 1956 at the Academy Awards and became a popular tune of the day. The film score by Bernard Herrmann, who had done the score for *The Trouble With Harry,* would make him part of the family, scoring many subsequent Hitchcock pictures.

In 1957 the film industry was having major problems trying to decide how to cope with its new rival, television. Warner Brothers owned the rights to a true story which appeared in *Life* magazine; and Hitchcock, feeling he could help out, decided to turn the property into a movie. He would take no salary for his work. Besides, he liked the project and he was in the mood to experiment once more.

His attention to detail and his desire to make the film as authentic as possible are part of the problems with this compelling but slow-moving film, *The Wrong Man.* The weight of the hero's problems is unrelenting, and even his acquittal isn't enough to counter the ponderous and depressing tone of this otherwise skillfully crafted picture.

"The True Story of Christopher Emmanuel Balestrero," by Maxwell Anderson, recounted the plight of the nightclub musician (Henry Fonda) who is falsely accused of armed robbery. A quiet and religious family man, he is sure that the police will discover their error and he'll soon be allowed to return to his home. The evidence, including closely matching handwriting on a robbery note and the positive identification of several witnesses, make his future look dim. His wife (Vera Miles) starts to lose her grip on reality, and she has to be confined

Hitchcock's fear of the police shows up again as an innocent Fonda is put through the demeaning arrest routine in The Wrong Man. (The Museum of Modern Art/Film Stills Archive)

to a sanatorium. Then the *real* thief is caught—a man who is an almost exact double for the accused. Fonda returns to his shattered life, with his wife the real victim of his false arrest.

The real facts of the case are minutely followed. Hitchcock interviewed many of the people involved and even used them in some of the film's scenes. Much of the film is shot on actual locations. Even the psychiatric rest home is the one in which the real Mrs.

Balestrero was committed, with the doctors playing themselves. Besides the careful handling of the subject, there are the brilliant performances by the leads, Henry Fonda and Vera Miles. Fonda, even though he was a major star at the time, is so natural and convincing as the plagued musician that the audience forgets he is performing a part. Vera Miles is equally realistic as the distraught wife and never approaches the melodrama most actresses would have attempted. Her transformation to her mental breakdown is slow and balanced, and she caps her performance in the scene where she tells her husband she doesn't wish to leave the sanatorium.

Fonda is acquitted when his double is arrested for the crime, but it is too late for Miles, who is committed to a sanitarium. Hitchcock strove for maximum authenticity. In this scene, an actual hospital and doctors are used.
(The Museum of Modern Art/Film Stills Archive)

"The television set now is like the toaster in American homes. You press a button and the same thing pops up . . . every time." —*Hitchcock*

Hitchcock hated the television medium, especially the commercials. That did not keep him from producing one of television's most successful series. *Alfred Hitchcock Presents* (initially produced for CBS). Why would an established movie director stoop to such an erstwhile unloved medium? Hitchcock was acutely aware of, and fully accepted, the commercial dictates of his profession. He never claimed to be a great artist; his goal was to work in his field as successfully as possible. When television's antennaed head loomed on the media horizon, many people in the film industry chose to ignore it by pretending that, by doing so, it would go away. Hitchcock and, most notably, the people who advised him perceived it differently and decided to strike while the cathode tube was still warming up.

The initiative came from Lew Wasserman, one of Hitchcock's closest friends and an important ally in his business ventures. Since 1945 Hitchcock had been represented by Wasserman and the firm he headed, MCA (Music Corporation of America). MCA was a multifaceted talent agency with branches in music publishing and motion picture production. Eventually they would become the parent corporation for Universal Pictures, a move that would add greatly to Hitchcock's wealth. It was 1955 when Wasserman urged Hitchcock to become involved in television, and Hitchcock's decision to comply would make him one of America's most memorable public figures.

Hitchcock's actual involvement in the series was limited. He formed a production company called Shamley

Productions (named after his old homestead in England), with Joan Harrison as the series' executive producer. Many of the Hitchcock regulars came aboard. Norman Lloyd, the villain in *Saboteur,* would take the job as assistant producer and would, one day, replace Joan Harrison. The show would attract top-notch writers such as Francis Cockrell and Ray Bradbury. Hitchcock himself directed 20 of the 365 episodes. But his contribution to the effort was primarily advice, script selection, and his inimitable introductions. More than anything, these deadpan openings helped lure the public into the brief tale of suspense and murder that followed. It was Hitchcock who first suggested the idea of his stepping into his own famous outline sketch and then appearing, often in costume, to deliver a brief bridge into the coming show. Almost always, he took jabs at the sponsor on these occasions.

These unrelenting attacks made him a hero to his viewers and to the sponsors for different reasons. In 1957 Hitchcock offered the *Saturday Evening Post* an explanation for his behavior. "The type of humor I wanted to use on television was the type I had employed in my film *The Trouble With Harry.* In that film, Harry was a dead body who was a 'botheration' to those who were alive. The awkward question, 'What'll we do with Harry?' was always popping up. There were those who found the notion gruesomely amusing; so I told myself that if no reverence to a [dead] body is amusing, no reverence for a live sponsor might be amusing, too."

The public concurred heartily, transforming Hitchcock into a TV cult figure. They relished his remarks on commercials, such as, "Most are deadly. They are perfect for my type of show;"

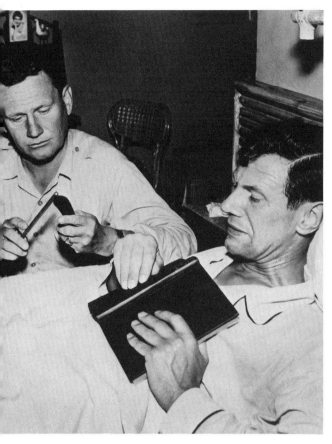

Hitchcock himself directed only 17 of the 365 episodes of Alfred Hitchcock Presents. *One of his efforts was "Poison." A terrified James Donald lies motionless while a deadly Malayan krait snake sleeps under the blanket on his stomach. Wendell Corey, who put it there, looks on laconically. (Memory Shop)*

and they roared at his appearances as Queen Victoria or with a hachet buried neatly in his head. "My guess is that my sponsor enjoys my lack of obsequiousness. But, in the beginning, they had [some] difficulty . . . getting used to my approach and . . . took umbrage at my less worshipful remarks," he said. "However, the moment they became aware of the commercial effects of my [technique]—they took a look at their sales charts—they stopped questioning the propriety of my cracks. There's no getting around it, I

did take getting used to. The tradition is that the sponsor must be coddled. In such an atmosphere, I was a novelty."

The production quality of his shows was uniformly good; utilizing good writers, actors, and storylines was rare in those days of early television. His show ranked alongside such classic series as *Playhouse 90* and *The Hallmark Hall of Fame.* Much of the success of the show fell on the selection of its material. It was a consistently lighthearted approach to serious subjects such as murder. He offered this theory on how he chose his material: "In selecting the stories for my television shows, I try to make them as meaty as the sponsor and the network will stand for. I hope to offset any tendency toward the macabre with humor. It's of a piece with such jokes as the one about the man who was being led to the gallows to be hanged. He looked at the trap door in the gallows, which was flimsily constructed, and he asked in some alarm, 'I say, is that thing safe?'"

Of the episodes he directed himself, many are considered the most memorable of the series. He did have first choice at the best scripts, so this is somewhat understandable. His first directing venture was "Breakdown," starring Joseph Cotten. Cotten plays a cruel businessman who is disgusted at the show of emotion by an employee when Cotten fires him. While on a road trip, Cotten is in an auto accident and pinned behind the wheel of his car. Everyone believes him dead, and he is first robbed and then thrown into a mortuary. The next morning, just as he is about to be pronounced dead and embalmed, a tear appears in his eye and he is taken to a hospital, where he recovers. Had it not been for his own tiny show of emotion, he would have been buried alive!

Hitchcock's TV show drew top-line talent, such as Jessica Tandy, seen here with Paul Playdon in "The Glass Eye." (Memory Shop)

"Revenge" was one of Hitchcock's favorites. Vera Miles plays the wife of an aircraft worker (Ralph Meeker) who has just returned from the hospital after a nervous breakdown. One day after work, Meeker finds her unconscious. When she recovers, she tells him she has been attacked. Fearing that the episode will cause her to be hospitalized again, Meeker takes their doctor's advice and they plan a vacation trip. But just as they are leaving, Miles spots her assailant and cries out, "That's the man, that's the man!" Meeker, filled with rage, follows him to his hotel room and beats him to death. He goes back to his wife and they start out again when she sees someone else and shouts, "That's

the man!" A shocked Meeker hears the police siren and realizes he had made a fatal error by believing her.

Hitchcock loved the absurd, and often his shows reflected this penchant. In "The Case of Mr. Pelham," starring Tom Ewell, a businessman is shocked to discover his exact double going about his own daily routines. He decides to outwit the impostor by wearing outrageous clothes and altering his own behavior. When the two finally confront each other, the *real* Mr. Pelham is pegged as a weirdo and carted off to a funny farm.

"Back for Christmas" featured John Williams as a wife killer. He buries her body in their basement and leaves for vacation. While he is away he finds out that his wife had planned to give him a wine cellar as a Christmas present. It is being excavated at that very moment in the basement where he secreted her body.

"Wet Saturday" starred Sir Cedric Hardwicke. It is a light piece with the usual simple plot. Hardwicke plays the father of a daughter who murders her boyfriend with a shovel. He tries to cover up his daughter's crime, but his irrational daughter winds up getting them both into hot water.

In "Mr. Blanchard's Secret" a nosy, suspicious housewife is sure that Mr. Blanchard has killed his wife. Then the viewer finds out Mr. Blanchard's *real* secret—he didn't do anything! The joke was on the housewife and, of course, Hitchcock's audience.

"One More To Go" has David Wayne as a successful wife killer. Here, Hitchcock plays off the suspense of getting caught to its fullest extent. Wayne stuffs his wife's body in the trunk of his car and drives to the country to bury it. A policeman stops him to point out that one of his taillights is faulty. After many excuses, the cop is about to open the trunk when the light comes back on. Wayne, grateful at his good fortune, drives off. But the cop decides to follow him, the light goes out again, and he insists it be repaired in the police garage.

"Four O'Clock" was the first episode of Hitchcock's hour-long series for NBC called *Suspicion.* He had already lengthened his series for CBS to be called *The Alfred Hitchcock Hour.* "Four O'Clock" was the tale of a watchmaker, played by E. G. Marshall, who believes his wife (Nancy Kelly) is being unfaithful. To get even, he plants a bomb in their house, but before he can leave, he is robbed by teenagers who bind and gag him and leave him in the basement with the hidden bomb. As the minutes tick by, a gas meter man and a little boy both come to the basement, but neither one detects his muffled cries. When the moment arrives, he's not killed—the electric power fails and the bomb is dormant.

At CBS, Hitchcock filmed "Perfect Crime" with Vincent Price and James Gregory. Price discovers that Gregory has condemned an innocent man to death, and neatly bakes him in a pottery kiln in revenge. Also at CBS, he directed his famous "Lamb to the Slaughter," starring Barbara Bel Geddes. This simple story probably served as an example for several unsolved crimes. Bel Geddes is upset that her husband is trying to leave her and bops him with a frozen leg of lamb. The blow kills him. Then, not knowing what to do with the lamb, she puts in in the oven and cooks it. When the police arrive, she invites them to join her for dinner while they discuss the disappearance of the murder weapon!

"Dip in the Pool" (CBS) is the only television show in which Hitchcock

Hitchcock drew much of the show's material from real crimes or stories that appeared in his magazine, Alfred Hitchcock Mystery Magazine. *Personally, he never read fiction, only contemporary biographies and travel books.* (Memory Shop)

makes a cameo appearance, á la *Lifeboat,* though as the cover picture on a magazine. In this tale, Keenan Wynn plays a sneaky swindler on a cruise with his wife (Fay Wray) and "Aunt Jenny's Four Thousand Dollars." He loses the money at cards but makes a wager to get it back, convincing the other guests to bet how far the ship will travel the next day. He bets on a low figure and gets a women to help him when he jumps off the boat, knowing that it will have to turn around when the woman calls for assistance. Unluckily, the woman is a mental patient and no one believes her tale of a "man overboard."

"Poison" is another tale of unbelief. It starred James McDonald as an alcoholic who is being murdered by a friend. The weapon used is a deadly snake which his friend places on his stomach. It will sleep as long as the intended victim remains motionless. When the victim discovers what is under the covers with him, he tries to explain his plight to others, but no one will believe him. He is left to suffer his fate with his friend waiting patiently by his bedside.

In "Banquo's Chair" (CBS), John Williams appears again as a police inspector who decides to trick a murderer into confession by having an actress play the part of the victim's ghost. The ghost appears and startles the murderer as planned, but almost immediately, the actress the detective had hired makes an entrance and apologizes for being tardy.

"Arthur" (CBS) returns to the problem of what to do with a dead spouse. Laurence Harvey, a single-minded farmer, refuses to marry Helen (Hazel Court). When she insists, he kills her, chops her up, and feeds her to his chickens. Perhaps Hitchcock was taking another slam at his dislike of

eggs—speculating on their possible contents!

"The Crystal Trench" (CBS) had the usual twist ending that came to characterize Hitchcock's shows. James Donald and Patricia Owens are a newly married couple and madly in love. She convinces him to go mountain climbing, where he falls into a deep glacier. She is told he will be visible forty years hence when the glacier moves down the mountain. Blaming herself for his death, she waits for the day she can see her deep-frozen husband once more. When the day finally arrives, she chips away at the ice and discovers not only her husband, but a locket he is wearing that contains a photograph of his secret lover.

"Incident at a Corner" (NBC) was a special presentation of *Ford Star Time,* directed by Hitchcock. This small-town drama examined the strange twists and turns a simple incident can take in such a setting. A school crossing guard has written a note admonishing the PTA president for reckless driving. The guard is fired when an unsigned note is received claiming that he is too friendly with the little girls at the school. It is made to appear as if the PTA president is trying to get even, but the villain of the piece turns out to be a woman living nearby. She knew the guard from another city and is afraid he will disclose her shady past.

Some of the Hitchcock television episodes are not at all concerned with murder, but take jabs at man's selfishness and greed. "Mrs. Bixby and the Colonel's Coat" (NBC) featured Audrey Meadows as an unfaithful wife. Her lover gives her a mink as a token of his esteem. She plans to get it into the house without her husband becoming suspicious. She pawns the fur and tells her husband she found the ticket. He

Joan Harrison was one of Hitchcock's most durable employees. She started with Hitchcock in 1935, quit to pursue her own producing career, and returned to produce the Alfred Hitchcock Presents *series.* (CBS Television Network)

offers to pick up the "free prize" for her, returning instead with a ratty old fur. Later, visiting her husband's office, she meets his secretary, who is wearing her own lover's expensive gift.

Claude Rains joined Hitchcock for "The Horseplayer" (NBC). Rains plays a priest looking for ways to make money for his parish. When he finds that a gambler is donating large sums of cash, he questions the man and finds out he makes church donations to bring him luck at the track. Rains decides to give the man several hundred dollars of the church building fund to bet, but subsequently feels so guilty about it that he prays for the horse to lose.

In the end, the horse wins, but the gambler had played the church money on the place position, so the priest's prayers are answered.

"Bang! You're Dead!" (NBC) was an hour-long piece starring child actor Billy Mumy. Mumy finds a loaded pistol and goes around pointing it at friends and family, saying "Bang!" No one notices the gun is real. Mumy always stops short of pulling the trigger, and when he finally does, the bullet strikes a wall. It is a simple plot, made excruciatingly tense by Hitchcock's expert direction.

"I Saw the Whole Thing" (CBS) was Hitchcock's last venture on television. It starred John Forsythe as the man accused of a hit-and-run accident that his wife committed. Several people claim to be witnesses, and the show demonstrates that when many people see the same thing, there will be many different versions.

The television series was not the only commercial enterprise to which Hitchcock lent his name. As the television show increased in popularity, Hitchcock approved the sale of several anthologies of short stories written by various people, but selected as being Hitchcock's in style and content. His profile appeared again on the monthly called *Alfred Hitchcock Mystery Magazine,* a pocket-sized publication that is still popular.

If all this was not making him rich enough, Hitchcock followed Lew Wasserman's advice and sold his interest in the series to Universal in 1964 in exchange for Universal stock. He could later look at the results of such directors as Steven Spielberg and know that even if he was being imitated, he at least was reaping some of those gargantuan profits earned by the new hotshot directors!

"There are no symbols in *North by Northwest*. Oh yes! The last shot. The train entering the tunnel after the love scene between Grant and Eva Marie Saint! It's a phallic symbol. But don't tell anyone!"—*Hitchcock*

Vertigo. North by Northwest. Psycho. The Birds. These four films are not only exemplary Hitchcock movies, but possibly four of the finest motion pictures he ever made. Each is a classic in its own right, but more important, they represent Hitchcock's creative high point, his best efforts to date. This is not to say that his previous work is in any way slighted. On the contrary, these works show the culmination of lessons he learned in such fine earlier works as *Strangers on a Train* and *The 39 Steps.* The marvelous thing about these works is that while they are all demonstrably Hitchcock films, they are unique from each other and show four different approaches to the realm of suspense filmmaking. Also, they are more pointedly watchful of the human comedy and tragedy than his earlier works.

Of the four, *Vertigo* is the best example of the humanistic approach, reminiscent of *Rear Window* in its probing analysis of human frailty.

The artistic merits of *Vertigo* are agreed on by many, most notably by two of Hitchcock's most ardent critics, Donald Spoto and Robin Wood. Wood, in his book *Hitchcock's Films,* states that *Vertigo* is "Hitchcock's most fully realized masterpiece . . . one of the four or five most profound and beautiful films the cinema has given us." Spoto, in his book *The Art of Alfred Hitchcock,* concurs unabashedly. He was so entranced by it that he has seen it twenty-six times and yearns for the opportunity to see it twenty-six more times!

The story is based on a novel by Pierre Boileau and Thomas Narcejac called *D'entre les Morts.* They also wrote

Vertigo is one of Hitchcock's finest films. James Stewart plays a detective who develops a terrible fear of heights after seeing a friend fall to his death. (Memory Shop)

a novel called *Les Diaboliques* which Hitchcock thought would make an excellent film. It was turned into a movie by the French director Clouest. Boileau and Narcejac, according to Truffaut, learned about Hitchcock's interest and set out to write a story especially for him to transfer to the screen. Hitchcock had not been aware of this previously and wondered aloud to Truffaut what the authors would have done if he hadn't purchased the property.

The initial draft of the screenplay was done by Alec Coppel, a British novelist and screenwriter. While he was at work, Hitchcock began to assemble his company. James Stewart accepted without even considering that it might not be a good vehicle for him. If Hitchcock asked, that was all Stewart needed to know. His choice for the role of Madeleine was Vera Miles, who was not as sophisticated a blonde as Hitchcock usually preferred but, he thought, an excellent actress.

Unfortunately, before filming began, Vera Miles withdrew because she was pregnant. Hitchcock was extremely disappointed and did not hide his feeling from the girl he chose to replace her— Kim Novak. On several occasions he took the opportunity to publicly discuss his dislike of the replacement, and informed the press that Novak was difficult and hard to get along with. Very possibly, she felt abused and therefore insecure, which would account for the fact that she gave Hitchcock some problems. Eventually he developed a working (and even somewhat of a private) relationship with her, even though he still believed Miles would have been better in the part. The screenwriter who completed the project, Sam Taylor, disagreed, saying to Donald Spoto, "The actress did not have the equipment to create two

In the first of a trio of great films, we see Hitchcock helping Jimmy Stewart select a gun for his part in Vertigo. *(Memory Shop)*

different people for the character of Madeleine and Judy. If we'd had a brilliant and famous actress who *could* create two roles, it might not have been as good. I am completely satisfied with her performance, because she seemed so completely naive—and therefore it was right." Spoto concurred, adding, "The casting of Kim Novak seems to me inspired. She is utterly credible, gives a luminous and, finally, a heart-breaking performance. It is in my opinion her best role."

Vertigo *ends with Stewart overcoming his fear of heights, but he is forced to watch Kim Novak fall from this tower, leaving him alone and desperate. The only real part of this shot is the stair Stewart is standing on—the rest is a studio miniature.* (The Museum of Modern Art/Film Stills Archive)

As it came time to start filming, Stewart and Hitchcock took a look at the script and found it totally unworkable. Samuel Taylor was called in to do a rewrite, from top to bottom without reading the novel. He found that much of the scenario was already in Hitchcock's mind, so he filled in the dialogue and added or expanded the characters. Indeed, Hitchcock had spent a great deal of time visualizing various scenes in *Vertigo,* and when it came time to plot the film, many pieces were already in place. What is most notable about the film is that Hitchcock had never been more meticulous in organizing the narrative and this attention to detail shows in every frame.

The movie begins as John Ferguson (James Stewart) watches a fellow detective fall to his death during a rooftop chase. The trauma causes him to develop acrophobia (fear of heights) which provokes his vertigo (a sensation of whirling about in space). Because of this, he elects to leave the police force. An old friend, Gavin Elster (Tom Helmore), asks him to do some private detective work for him. Helmore wants Stewart to trail his wife, Madeleine (Kim Novak), who, he claims, is suicidal. Stewart follows her and finds himself falling in love. When she attempts to drown herself in San Francisco Bay, he saves her. Later, he is guilt-ridden when she goes up a church tower and hurls herself off. Because of his vertigo, he could not follow her. He takes refuge with his former girl friend, Midge (Barbara Bel Geddes), who nurses him back to health from a near nervous breakdown. Then, some months later, Stewart meets a young girl who is an exact double for Madeleine. She insists she has never met him before nor heard of Madeleine. Obsessed with the idea of having rediscovered Madeleine, he urges the young girl to dress like her.

Following his theory that there is more suspense if the audience knows the truth, Hitchcock flashes back to a scene which reveals that Judy and Madeleine are indeed the same person. Judy, it turns out, is his old friend's mistress and was only playacting Madeleine. She lured Stewart to the church tower knowing he couldn't follow her in order to furnish a witness to the real Madeleine's death by "suicide." It is, of course, a case of homicide.

Stewart confirms the truth when Judy inadvertently wears a necklace she had worn as Madeleine. Desperate with rage, he forces her to the church tower to get her to confess. In the process, he overcomes his vertigo, but she hears someone coming, and, startled, falls to her death. The movie ends with Stewart, trapped by the impending return of his illness, gazing down from the height.

It is a complicated psychological plot, with puzzling twists and turns that are never quite explained. Hitchcock refers to these often-illogical moments as "icebox talk" scenes, meaning that they will be discussed and dissected by the audience while they are scouting the icebox for leftovers after the movie is over.

With a lighter touch in mind, Hitchcock proceeded to create his comic thriller *North by Northwest,* the only film he made for MGM. He started to work with screenwriter Ernest Lehman on a story about a boat sailing on the English Channel with only one person aboard, to be titled *The Wreck of the Mary Deare.* When it became obvious that the project was not going to work out for him, he moved on to *North by Northwest.*

North by Northwest *is Hitchcock's only MGM film and a great classic comedy thriller.* (The British Film Institute/National Film Archive/Stills Library)

In trying to come up with an unusual way to have someone killed, Hitchcock created this classic scene of terror—a man trapped in the wide open spaces of an Illinois cornfield being chased by a crop duster in North by Northwest. (The Museum of Modern Art/Film Stills Archive)

The plot for North by Northwest *was so compli-cated that Grant and others in the cast often had no idea why they were doing a particular scene.* (The Museum of Modern Art/Film Stills Archive)

Again, the intense planning is profoundly evident in the complex and carefully realized plot. *North by Northwest* is reminiscent of his earlier chase adventures. In place are the now-familiar Hitchcock building blocks: a cool but vulnerable blonde (Eva Marie Saint), a favorite major leading man (Cary Grant, in his fourth and final Hitchcock role), and a "MacGuffin," a piece of African art with secrets hidden inside it.

The story line may be one of the most complicated Hitchcock devised for the screen. Grant plays an advertising executive named Roger Thornhill. He is mistaken for an imaginary agent the CIA invented in order to smoke out enemy spies, George Kaplan, and is captured by the enemy. He manages

to escape, and fails to convince the police and his mother (Jessie Royce Landis) he had been kidnapped. He is then accused of killing a UN diplomat and escapes on a train headed for Chicago. On board, he meets Eve Kendall (Eva Marie Saint), who works for the enemy. He is told he can meet the real Kaplan (a ploy by the enemy) in a cornfield in Illinois. There he is attacked by a crop-dusting biplane. He makes it back to Chicago and finds Eve and her spy-lover, Vandamm (James Mason) at an art auction (buying the African piece). He escapes their clutches by getting arrested for disturbing the peace and is taken to the airport, where the CIA project director (Leo G. Carroll) explains what is going on; that is, that there is no spy named Kaplan and that Saint is a double agent. Grant agrees to play out the role of the spy in order to protect Saint. What follows is an incredible chase scene

In the breathtaking finale, Eva Marie Saint and Cary Grant are trapped on Mount Rushmore. At one point Hitchcock considered filming this scene on location, but used a studio mock-up for safety reasons. (The Museum of Modern Art/Film Stills Archive)

across the Mount Rushmore monument, culminating in a victorious train ride home that gives rise to Hitchcock's quote on the sexual context of the film's last shot.

The movie's twists and turns in the plot nearly drove the cast crazy during filming. Grant complained he couldn't figure out what was going on and he doubted if the audience would fare any better. There are many similarities to some of Hitchcock's earlier work—particularly *The 39 Steps,* with its elaborate chase sequence, and *Saboteur,*

which also has the villain and hero battling on a national monument. But there are several original touches, too.

Comedy is most evident in the first part of the film. In one scene, Grant is forced to consume a bottle of bourbon and taken out to be killed. He manages to gain control of the car, and there is a funny, exciting scene of him out-maneuvering the bad guys. He is arrested for his erratic escapade but no one believes his story, including his mother. In another sequence, Grant and his mother are on an elevator with the two men who are trying to kill him. He identifies them as murderers and his mother thinks the remark is amusing, even asking the thugs, "You two aren't really trying to kill my son, are you?" causing her, the thugs, and everyone else in the elevator (but Grant) to start laughing.

The climax is one of the most suspenseful movie chases, as Grant and Saint slip-slide over the stone faces of Mount Rushmore. This scene, actually filmed on studio reconstruction, is the epitome of terror. Similarly, Hitchcock, confronted with another scene of his hero being pursued by someone with murderous intent, thought first of the obvious: a dark alley, a rainy night, and the slow approach of a black limousine. Instead, he reversed the cliché. A daylighted, barren cornfield in Illinois. The scene begins with Grant stepping off a bus at a spot where there is nothing in sight for miles. In the distance, we can faintly detect the sound and shape of a small airplane. Soon Grant realizes there are no crops in the fields! What is a crop duster doing there? Then the plane attacks. It is a harrowing moment as Grant finds himself trapped in the wide open spaces.

North by Northwest was a creative and commercial triumph, and it

remains popular to this day. The color is superb, the plot engrossing, and the casting excellent. It is Hitchcock's longest picture, running 136 minutes. MGM felt strongly that it ought to be trimmed to a much shorter running time, but fortunately, his agent, MCA, had a clause in his contract which gave him complete artistic control. He gratefully exercised his option and kept his film intact.

"You have to remember that *Psycho* is a film made with quite a sense of amusement on my part. To me, it's a fun picture. The process through which we take the audience, you see, [is] rather like taking them through the haunted house at the fairground," said Hitchcock of his next feature.

Psycho is an unprecedented combination of suspense, terror, and violence. It is not classic Hitchcock, but it has been listed by several critics as one of the ten best movies of all time. Yet at one point, Hitchcock almost lost faith in it and was prepared to run it on his television series instead of releasing it to the theaters.

In John Russell Taylor's biography on Hitchcock, he points out that at this time, 1960, the low-budget horror film was becoming a Hollywood staple. Hitchcock began to wonder what he would do with such a genre. Although *Psycho* was produced under the auspices of Paramount, he personally financed the project. His goal was to make it as cheaply as possible. It was realized with a total outlay of eight

Psycho, *according to Hitchcock, was a fun picture, like going through a haunted house. He set out to make a great, inexpensive horror film and ended up with one of the best movies ever—and for a mere eight hundred thousand dollars.* (The Museum of Modern Art/Film Stills Archive)

Hitchcock had a dry, often bizarre sense of humor. Here he is cavorting on the set of Psycho. (The British Film Institute/National Film Archive/ Stills Library)

Psycho *was daring for a 1960 film—the opening scene shows Janet Leigh in her bra. Hitchcock insisted that no one enter the theater after the movie began.* (The Museum of Modern Art/ Film Stills Archive)

The house above the motel, where Tony Perkins and his mother lived, was a standing Universal set: a typical Gothic horror house. Hitchcock used it subtly and showed very little of the interior.
(The Museum of Modern Art/Film Stills Archive)

hundred thousand dollars. (It has since made more than twenty million dollars). He used his television production staff, as many standing sets as possible, and watched his pennies when he cast for actors. At that time Anthony Perkins was a popular star and Hitchcock's first choice as the boyish killer. Luckily, Perkins owed Paramount a movie and was obtained for the role at a relatively low figure for someone of his stature. Vera Miles was under a personal contract to Hitchcock, and Janet Leigh was not terribly expensive. He needed a major star for the role so that her death, early in the film, would come as a shock to the audience. The decision worked out beautifully.

The plot is simple but effective. The story opens with Marion (Janet Leigh) and her lover, Sam (John Gavin), sharing an afternoon. They want to get married, but neither can afford it. Marion is given forty thousand dollars by her boss to deposit, but she steals the money and leaves town. After taking a wrong turn in the rain, she stops at a small motel and asks for a room. The owner, Norman Bates (Anthony Perkins), is a lonely soul and tells her that he lives up the hill in an old mansion with his mother, a domineering invalid. After Norman leaves, she decides to take a shower. Suddenly the old lady appears and stabs her to death. Norman finds the body in the shower and proceeds to cover up his mother's handiwork; he hides the body in the trunk of Leigh's car and pushes it into a nearby pond.

Leigh's sister Lia (Vera Miles) and Gavin hire a private detective to

105

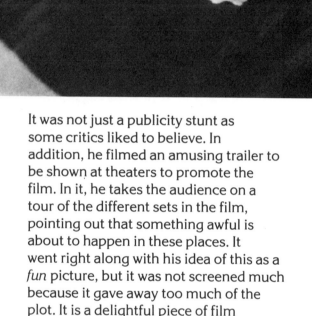

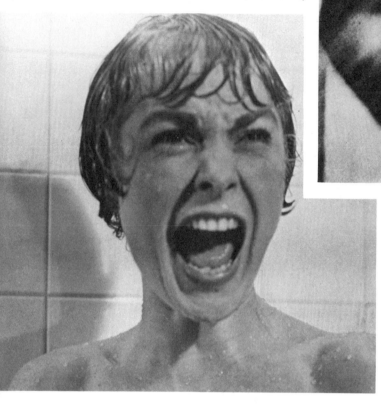

The famous shower scene from Psycho. *It took a week to film and contains seventy-eight separate shots. The knife never touches flesh, nor is it seen with blood on it. The film remains one of the most talked-about films of the sixties.* (The Museum of Modern Art/ Film Stills Archive)

find the money. The detective traces her to the motel and goes up to the Bates house, where he is attacked by the knife-wielding mother on the stairwell. Miles and Gavin try to involve the local sheriff, but he tells them that Perkin's mother has been dead for some time. They go to the motel, where Miles discovers the horrible truth. She comes upon the mummified body of Mrs. Bates. Norman, a psychopath, thinks he *is* his mother and has committed many murders disguised as her.

The twist ending and the early death of Janet Leigh caused Hitchcock to insist that no one be allowed to enter the theater after the show began.

It was not just a publicity stunt as some critics liked to believe. In addition, he filmed an amusing trailer to be shown at theaters to promote the film. In it, he takes the audience on a tour of the different sets in the film, pointing out that something awful is about to happen in these places. It went right along with his idea of this as a *fun* picture, but it was not screened much because it gave away too much of the plot. It is a delightful piece of film nonetheless.

In *Psycho,* Hitchcock took several chances he had not taken before. Even more unlike Hitchcock than the explicit sexual scene at the film's opening was the explicit violence. Until *Psycho,* Hitchcock's films carefully avoided blatant violence. Murder was never seen, but implied. He stuck close to this theory, but proceeded to give the world one of its most violent film scenes. The shower murder provoked many outrageous reactions. Hitchcock gave this example: "Most of my fans are highly intelligent people per se, or they wouldn't be watching my shows. Some, however, are idiots. One man wrote to me, after I had Janet Leigh murdered in a bathtub in *Psycho,* that his wife had been afraid to bathe or shower since seeing the film. He asked me for suggestions as to what he should do. I wrote back, 'Sir, have you considered sending your wife to be drycleaned?'"

In order to keep the violence of the shower scene to a minimum, *Psycho* was filmed in black and white. Hitchcock felt the red of the blood would be too much! As violent as the stabbing appears, the *knife never touches flesh.* Nor is it seen with blood on it, for that matter. Rather than hold the camera on the scene, there is a startling montage of the victim, the knife, and the blood. The one minute of film took one week of filming, with seventy-eight separate shots. A special shower was built with a platform around it so that Hitchcock could stand above it and direct. Much of the filming itself was done without the benefit of either Leigh or Perkins. In fact, Perkins was not even there when the scene was shot. Furthermore, Hitchcock did not think it proper for Leigh to be filmed nude, so only shots of her face and hands are seen, and a model was hired for the other brief glimpses of skin. The finale to the sequence is arresting as Leigh slumps over the edge of the tub, her face to the floor as the camera closes in on her eyes. At this point, when the movie was being screened for Alma and Hitchcock, Alma raised an objection: She pointed out that she saw Leigh swallow. Anyone else would have been too stunned by the preceding action to notice, but not Hitchcock's most professional critic. The shot was immediately corrected.

At this point, Hitchcock had scored mightily with three very different films. One was a psychological drama, one a comic suspense movie, and the last, a horror film. He added to this lineup his only venture into science fiction with *The Birds.*

"*The Birds* is coming!" was Hitchcock's own contribution to the publicity effort. It was an unusual venture for Hitchcock not only in content, but in the heavy dependence on special technical effects. He was always aware of and involved with special effects (such as the Shuftan process) but he had never allowed them to dominate before. But things were changing in the movie business and Hitchcock, his finger ever on his industry's pulse. sensed a movement toward technically elaborate pictures. As usual, it was a prophetic impulse.

The script for *The Birds* was adapted by Evan Hunter from Daphne du Maurier's short story of the same title. The tale came to his attention in one of the anthologies published under his name. He had always had a fascination with birds as threatening creatures. There was something about their frantic, uncontrolled behavior and their ability to appear from above that made them menacing. In the analysis of the filming of *The Birds* in the magazine *Cinefantastique,* Kyle Counts quotes Hitchcock as saying, "Birds made excellent heavies. After all, they've been put in cages, shot, and shoved in ovens for centuries. It's only natural that they should fight back."

It is a fairly simple story. Melanie Daniels (Tippi Hedren) and Mitch Brenner (Rod Taylor) meet in a pet shop in San Francisco. She is cold and indifferent, but doesn't ignore his advances. He buys two lovebirds as a present for his little sister, and she delivers them to him at his home on Bodega Bay. En route, she is attacked by a sea gull, which grazes her forehead.

107

The Birds *was Hitchcock's most complicated movie technically. He spent two hundred thousand dollars trying to develop mechanical birds, but wound up using the real thing. "It makes me tired just watching them. Thank goodness I'm only paying them birdseed." (The Museum of Modern Art/Film Stills Archive)*

Hitchcock spent months planning this film. The Birds *required an enormous crew and was filmed mostly on location. (The British Film Institute/National Film Archive/ Stills Library)*

There are 370 different trick shots in The Birds. *In this scene, schoolchildren flee from the flying menace. The birds were added later through the optical printing process. (Memory Shop)*

near Bodega school.

437 melanie - Run - Run.

440 children (foregrnd against Sodium screen) Background Bodega school with michelle and 2 or 3 children

440A continuation of 440. - melanie runs past camera

Art - 12

The Birds *was the most difficult of Hitchcock's movies to storyboard. This continuity sketch was numbered and used to keep track of each individual shot.* (The Museum of Modern Art/Film Stills Archive)

The attic scene attack on
Tippi Hedren took a week to film.
She endured hundreds of birds being
thrown at her and tied to her body.
Finally, a sea gull nearly took
out her eye and she ran screaming
from the set. (The Museum of Modern
Art/Film Stills Archive)

The original ending was to
have Rod Taylor and his family
leave Bodega Bay and cross
the Golden Gate Bridge,
horrified to see it covered with
birds. Instead, Hitchcock
ended the movie as they left their
house. Here he is seen directing
his feathered acting company.
(The British Film Institute/National
Film Archive/Stills Library)

110

She decides to spend the night. Taylor's little sister has a birthday party the next day, and the children are unexpectedly attacked by more gulls. Later that evening the Brenner house is inundated with sparrows. The following morning, the first victim is found—a local farmer who has been pecked to death.

The threat grows as a huge flock of crows tries to storm a local school-house. Hedren manages to usher the children to safety but the schoolteacher (Suzanne Pleshette) is killed at her home. That night the Brenner house is attacked by scores of birds trying to enter. They decide to leave Bodega Bay, and as they do so, swarms of birds peacefully watch them leave.

Hitchcock never explains why the birds have decided to take over, seeing no reason to get into complicated scientific explanations that would distract from the story. Privately, he maintained that it was some form of rabies. He always felt that there were a lot of weaknesses in *The Birds,* especially the script. He told Kyle Counts, "Like all pictures of this nature, its personality didn't carry. If the picture seemed less powerful in 1975 than it did in 1963, that's the main reason, that the personal story was weak. But don't tell that to Evan Hunter."

Hunter was not Hitchcock's first choice to write the screenplay. He first offered the job to Ray Bradbury, but Bradbury was writing for the television series at the time and told Hitchcock, "I have this other employer— *you*—and you must wait for you to unemploy me in order for me to write *The Birds.*" Hitchcock couldn't wait. Later, Bradbury regretted his haste, saying, "He would have had a better screenplay. Much of the film he wound up with was a bore. Some parts, of course, are brilliant. But I don't like the finale, and I think I might have, just might have, done better."

Nevertheless, there is a memorable amount of terror in the bird attacks, which constituted a major technical problem. Hitchcock hoped to use mechanical birds and process shots. Two hundred thousand dollars were invested in developing fake birds, but virtually none were used, so, bird trainer Ray Berwick was brought in to organize the real thing. A number of complicated process shots were used, a detailed analysis of which is presented in the fall 1980 issue of *Cinefantastique.*

One of Berwick's biggest chores was the bird attack on Hedren in the attic room. For one minute of film, seven days of exhausting shooting were required. Originally Hedren was told that they would be using mechanical birds, but when she stepped onto the set the first day of shooting, there was a huge cage built around the set. Two technicians were poised with heavy gloves on, prepared to hurl hundreds of birds at her. It was a brutal ordeal for the actress, but it was her first film and she didn't think she could refuse. As filming progressed, she became more and more nervous at having the birds thrown at her or tied to her. Finally, on the last day, a gull nearly took her eye out. No one was surprised when she ran screaming from the set.

The critics were not as satisfied with *The Birds* as they had been with his previous three films. Hitchcock tended to agree, but it remains a popular movie to this day and is shown with more frequency than the others.

If he had not been so proficient on these pictures, his next five might not have appeared as dismal. In all, his last five films reflect his growing ill health and a consequent inability to make sound artistic judgments.

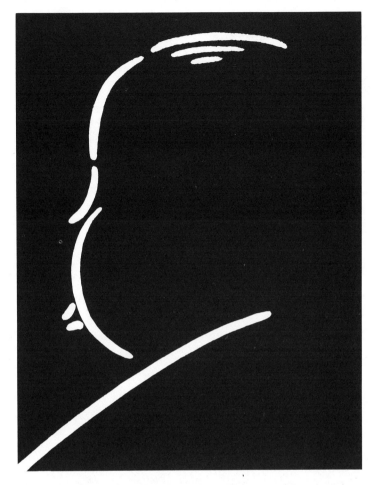

"People constantly ask me, 'Why are you so interested in crime?' The truth is, I'm not. I'm only interested in it as it affects my profession. I won't even drive a car for fear I will get a ticket. The thought that if I drove I would face that possibility day after day frightens me horribly, for I can't bear suspense."

—*Hitchcock*

 If not personally interested in crime and how crime affected his own life, Hitchcock was certainly interested in how it affected others. He made this concern the theme of his 1964 picture, *Marnie*. Marnie Edgar (Tippi Hedren) is sexually frigid and transfers her hatred of men into a succession of robberies. Her pattern consists of gaining the confidence of an employer and then pilfering the company. Her nefarious career forces her to move after each robbery to a different city. And besides being unable to cope with men, she is terrified by the color red and by thunderstorms. Her illegal career runs into a snag when she gets a job with Mark Rutland (Sean Connery), who knows she is a thief. His obsession is that he is attracted to women who steal. When he catches her trying to rob his safe, he asks her to marry him or he'll send her to prison. She reluctantly consents, and the ensuing marriage night causes her to attempt suicide. She tries to rob his safe again, but is unable to go through with it. Eventually Connery learns that she is not the orphan she professed, and believing she needs to confront her phobias, he forces her to visit her mother. She discovers that her mother was a prostitute and that at the age of five, Hedren killed a sailor who was trying to hurt her. The other phobias are explained away and the film ends with the impression that her new husband will help her work them out.

Part of the problem with Marnie *was the shoddy special effects. In this scene, Tippi Hedren rides a fake horse against a fake process-background.* (The Museum of Modern Art/Film Stills Archive)

Marnie was a total disaster at the box office, and the critics were mixed in their opinions. Some critics still feel that it is a darkly melancholy but flawed film; while others considered it one of Hitchcock's worst. Many of its detractors complain of the sloppy technical effects in the process shots, where the backgrounds are often shoddy and blurred. In one particularly bad case, Hedren is seen riding an obviously fake horse against an equally phony moving background. When confronted with these objections, Hitchcock confessed that he was rushed —an unusual excuse for him.

The favorable reactions are in part based on a smattering of interesting

camera work and the complicated character motivations. Everyone seemed to agree that it was an ill-conceived project and not like Hitchcock to allow so much dialogue. People began to comment that Hitchcock was showing signs of age; that he was not capable of making great movies anymore.

Torn Curtain told the story of an American scientist (Paul Newman) who pretends to defect in order to learn an important scientific formula from an East German professor. His fiancée (Julie Andrews) decides to follow him, not knowing he is bluffing. Newman is forced to kill an agent who discovers his motive, and he must quietly get the formula out of the country. He winds up explaining everything to Andrews, who helps him escape with the secret.

Hitchcock's decision to use big names is largely responsible for the dreary reception of this film. Julie Andrews was not at all a Hitchcock

The most memorable scene in Torn Curtain *was the realistic death scene. Hitchcock wanted to show how hard it is to kill someone. Newman starts by stabbing and then trying to strangle Wolfgang Kieling.* (The Museum of Modern Art/Film Stills Archive)

Then, with the help of Carolyn Conwell, he ends up stuffing the man into an oven and gassing him to death. (The British Film Institute/National Film Archive/Stills Library)

MR. HITCHCOCK

heroine, nor was Paul Newman a Hitchcock hero. The picture opens with them in bed, much like the opening of *Psycho*. Their performances go downhill thereafter. Hitchcock had particular problems with Newman, another method actor. In his previous encounters with actors who had to "feel" the part from within (Montgomery Clift and Vera Miles) there was a mutual understanding which was achieved. Not so with Newman: he refused to follow Hitchcock's directions and even managed to insult him by insisting on drinking a beer out of the can when invited to Hitchcock's house for dinner.

Significantly, Hitchcock accepted screen violence in this film. He felt that if you have to do it, do it right. He had always been bothered by the ease with which people in the movies died. One shot, a clout on the head, or a thrust of a knife is all it usually took. Hitchcock set out to show a more grimly realistic approach, with Newman trying to kill the East German agent —first by stabbing him, but the knife breaks off in his shoulder; then by strangulation, but he's too strong and large-necked. A woman tries to help by bashing the man with a shovel, which only succeeds in getting him down on the floor. Once there, Newman *and* the woman manage to drag the struggling victim to an oven, where they hold his face over a gas jet until he finally expires.

Generally, the reception for *Topaz* was not much better than *Torn Curtain*. Why Hitchcock decided to do another of these un-Hitchcock-like films is not known. Neither had the usual suspense elements, and both were made quickly without benefit of his careful preplanning. Much of *Topaz* (written by

Samuel Taylor) was scripted days before shooting, a system Hitchcock detested in spite of the fact it was based on the popular novel by Leon Uris.

Andre Devereaux (Frederick Stafford) is a French diplomat helping the CIA learn about Russia's activities in Cuba. Stafford and his wife (Dany Robin) are at odds over his suspected affair with his Cuban contact (Karin Dor), who is killed by the Cubans. The rest of the picture involves Stafford and his American CIA contact trying to smoke out a French official who is selling secrets to the Russians.

It is an awkward and wordy film with little to hold audience interest. The color is good and it is used effectively in one memorable sequence: Karin Dor's death. Her lover has found out she is a traitor as he is holding her in his arms. He speaks softly, telling her he knows she will be tortured for her crime and he can't bear the thought. He slips his gun behind her and there is a sharp report. The camera moves directly overhead as they stand together on a black-and-white checkerboard marble floor. She falls, her brilliant purple dress flowing around her like a blossom opening. It is a stunning, if brief, effect achieved by putting wire spokes in the gown, which opened as she collapsed to the floor.

Things looked grim for Hitchcock. The public was convinced he'd lost his touch, and the critics were finding him difficult to defend. Then in 1972 he decided to return to London to film *Frenzy*.

Frenzy is not great Hitchcock, but it is good Hitchcock. The critics rushed to herald the master's return, and the box office kept busy as patrons lined up to enjoy his latest entertainment. Much of *Frenzy* is a return to form:

Hitchcock directing Karin Dor's death scene in Topaz; *it is the most memorable scene in the picture.* (Memory Shop)

Frenzy *marked Hitchcock's return to form. He*
filmed it in London and drew crowds of fans as
he cavorted with his dummy, who was originally
slated to make his cameo appearance floating
down the Thames, but was yanked because
Hitchcock felt it looked too fake on film.
(The Museum of Modern Art/Film Stills Archive/The
British Film Institute/National Film Archive/
Stills Library)

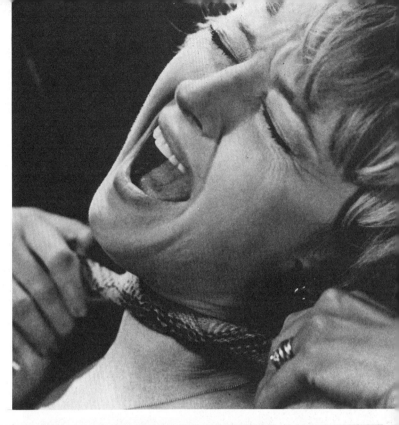

Frenzy was Hitchcock's most violent film and the only one to be rated R. Barbara Leigh-Hunt has just been raped and is now being brutally strangled to death. (The Museum of Modern Art/ Film Stills Library)

There is the wrong man accused of a crime, an appealing villain, an unpleasant hero, and several comic touches to keep the pressure off the audience. It is also Hitchcock's only R-rated picture. He conceded to popular taste, presenting as explicit a murder scene as he had ever done, one that contained some nudity.

The script is tight, thanks to British playwright Anthony Shaffer, who adapted the story from Arthur Labern's novel, *Goodbye Piccadilly, Farewell Leicester Square.* Richard Blaney (Ron Finch) is a rough ex-RAF pilot who is fired from his bartending job for stealing drinks. He tells his troubles to his successful produce-dealer friend, Bob Rusk (Barry Foster), and then goes to see his ex-wife at her matrimonial agency, where they have a fight. The next day Foster goes to see her, brutally rapes her, and strangles her with his necktie.

Of course the husband, Finch, is suspected of the crime, as well as many similar crimes committed in the area. He is helped in eluding capture by his girl friend (Anna Massey). He finds a friend to stay with, but she keeps a tryst with Foster, who rapes and kills her, too. Foster hides her body in a potato sack and sends her off in a truck. Only later, he realizes she has an incriminating piece of evidence on her, and he must find the body to retrieve it. Finch has gone to Foster for help, but Foster double-crosses him, and Finch gets convicted of the crimes. A police inspector (Alec McGowan) decides to check out Finch's claim of

When the killer (played by Barry Foster) finds out that the body in the potato sack has his tiepin, he is compelled to retrieve it from her deathgrip. The snap of each finger as it is broken open is an excruciating Hitchcock touch. (The British Film Institute/National Film Archive/Stills Library)

119

innocence, and, when things look darkest, McGowan reveals the true killer.

It is a skillfully plotted and photographed movie with a bright English cast; a delightful blend of the funny and the frightening. Alec McGowan is deftly amusing as he tries to solve the crime and put up with his wife's (Vivien Merchant) newfound love for gourmet cooking. His expressions, as he tries to tell his wife what he's found out about the murder case while attempting to eat overcooked quail, are sublime.

Later, Hitchcock makes a simple

scene excruciating as Foster tries to retrieve his incriminating tiepin from the death grip of his latest victim. First he must dig her body out of the potato sack in the back of a moving truck. Then he finds the pin locked in her frozen fingers. Slowly, he breaks each finger to regain the pin. The snap of the digits is like a jolt to the spine.

During filming of his fifty-third and final feature, *Family Plot,* Hitchcock suffered a heart attack and had a pacemaker installed. He bounced back from his surgery, delighted to show his scar and relate how he had it done with a local anesthetic so he could watch the operating procedure. He took his time getting the script together, with Ernest Lehman adapting from Victor Canning's novel, *The Rainbird Pattern.*

Barbara Harris and Bruce Dern play a couple of swindlers. Harris

William Devane was told to behave like William Powell and let the clothes do the acting. Karen Black describes Hitchcock as "having an inner placidity. He always thinks of his audience and how it will respond." (Memory Shop)

Ever the ham, Hitchcock threw a press party for Family Plot, *replete with horse-drawn hearse and gravestones with the reporters' names inscribed on them.* (The Museum of Modern Art/Film Stills Archive)

pretends to have psychic powers and relies on Dern to get her the real facts in order to impress her customers so she can bilk them. When an old lady (Cathleen Nesbitt) asks her to find her illegitimate nephew so that she can make him rich, Harris and Dern try to oblige—for a price. The nephew (William Devane) turns out to be a jewel thief, assisted by Karen Black. He kidnaps famous people and exchanges them for large diamonds. As the film progresses, Harris and Dern get close to finding out Devane's identity, but he isn't aware of why they are after him and he tries to kill them, suspecting they know his real occupation. In the end, the villains are caught and Harris and Dern get their reward.

Hitchcock's fascination with the improbable was the basis for one of the film's better scenes. Devane and Black have decided to kidnap a bishop. Rather than do it at night, they commit their crime in broad daylight while the bishop is officiating mass. It is a deft and realistic scene: Hitchcock plays on the idea of a church congregation not believing such a thing could happen and being too polite to do anything to prevent it.

Hitchcock started work with Ernest Lehman on a screenplay for his next picture. But, by November 1979 he had become so ill that he could no longer receive mail or visitors. His death came as a shock to his public—but then he always did like to keep them in suspense.

"Sex has never interested me much. I don't understand how people can waste so much time over sex. Sex is for kids, for movies; [it is] a great bore." —*Hitchcock*

 Hitchcock was a very private, candid man. It seems, at first glance, that such a remark would be out of character for him, but then he did make it. He also was very frank that he was virgin husband at twenty-seven and began a life of celibacy at the age of forty-two. As he states in the quote, he recognized sex as an integral part of a film; a necessary evil, but not a subject to be ignored, no matter his own feelings. His theories on what constituted sexual attraction were as clearly defined as his other filmic ideas. How his predilections came about has never been explained. He liked blondes—cool, quiet, and utterly controlled blondes that he could manipulate on the screen and often reduce to an emotional wreck. He explained his theory to Truffaut. "You know why I favor sophisticated blondes in my films? We're after the drawing-room type, the real ladies, who become whores once they're in the bedroom."

His penchant for this type of blonde goes back to *The Manxman,* his 1929 silent that starred Anny Ondra, who also appeared in *Blackmail.* She came across the screen as at once childlike and playful, and passionate and desperate. He and Alma both enjoyed her company and they were close personal friends. He loved to tease her, which is clear in the following text of a voice test she did for him that is on file at the British Film Institute.

Hitchcock: Now, Miss Ondra, we are going to do a sound test. Isn't that what you wanted? Now come right over here.
Anny Ondra: I don't know what to say. I'm so nervous.
Hitchcock: Have you been a good girl?
Anny Ondra: (Laughing) Oh, no.

Hitchcock: No? Have you slept with men?
Anny Ondra: No!
Hitchcock: No?!
Anny Ondra: Oh, Hitch, you make me so embarrassed! (Begins to laugh uncontrollably.)
Hitchcock: Now come over here and stand in your place, or it won't come out right, as the girl said to the soldier. (She walks off laughing)
Hitchcock: (Grinning) Cut!

This flirtatious behavior was conducted openly and was no more than what it appeared to be—the playful attentions of a man for a girl he admired and for whom he had no amorous intentions. Hitchcock, ever the pragmatist, probably assumed that none of these girls were going to find him physically attractive, but he could at least be charming. And he was, as long as possible. But if they ever tried to meddle with his directions on the set, they were confronted with his brusque side, the same as anyone.

The importance of looking at how Hitchcock felt about women is that it best shows his humanity. Not only did women figure prominently in his films, but they were his closest friends and allies. Two women in particular were, at different times, his right hand. Joan Harrison was pert, blonde, and a language student at Cambridge when she answered an advertisement for a secretary. This was just prior to the making of *The 39 Steps,* and she had no idea for whom she was interviewing. Hitchcock took an instant liking to her and hired her on the spot. She picked up more and more know-how about the movie business, until she eventually became his closest production associate. She is credited with being involved with many of his scripts, usually

Anny Ondra, Hitchcock's first blonde heroine, was a type he was very fond of and certainly sought for his movies. Here Hitchcock is rehearsing Ondra for a sound test in Blackmail. (The British Film Institute/National Film Archive/Stills Library)

working in tandem with Alma. It is important to note that these women became not only Hitchcock's confidantes, but Alma's as well. They both seemed to enjoy encouraging and developing these bright young women and made them part of their family. Joan Harrison would stay with Hitchcock for seven years, until she branched out on her own. Later she would return to Hitchcock as the executive producer of his television series.

His next discovery was another young Englishwoman he first hired as a continuity girl for *Under Capricorn,* Peggy Robertson, who remained connected with Hitchcock until the time of his death.

The next significant blonde actress was Madeleine Carroll in *The 39 Steps* and *Secret Agent.* Carroll was already successful as a performer and not so susceptible to Hitchcock's charm. However, when Hitchcock had her pulled through muddy streams and shoved around in handcuffs in *The 39 Steps,* she accepted the challenge like a trouper and earned Hitchcock's and his crew's respect.

With *Rebecca* came Joan Fontaine. She was correct for the part, but still

Joan Fontaine was having trouble with Laurence
Olivier in Rebecca. Hitchcock knew this
and became, as she described it, "too protective."
Here she is in a scene with Nigel Bruce from
the film. (Memory Shop)

Carole Lombard asked Hitchcock to direct her in
Mr. and Mrs. Smith, which proved to be a
mistake. She was a good friend and they shared
a similar puckish sense of humor. (The Museum
of Modern Art/Film Stills Archive)

not the highly sophisticated blonde Hitchcock would fashion later. He was personally concerned about her, and went out of his way to encourage his sponsorship. During filming, her relations with Laurence Olivier were strained, as Olivier was disappointed that his wife, Vivian Leigh, was not cast in the film. Hitchcock took it upon himself to shelter Fontaine from Olivier's obvious dislike. She complained, "He protected me; wouldn't let anyone near me. He kept me in a cocoon." Often his leading ladies would react in this way—that he was too paternal and protective. But Joan Fontaine became famous in *Rebecca,* and Hitchcock used her again in *Suspicion,* for which she would receive an Oscar.

In between *Rebecca* and *Suspicion,* he made *Mr. and Mrs. Smith* with Carole Lombard. Here was a blonde he adored for her strength of character and strong sense of humor. She and her husband, Clark Gable, were good friends to the Hitchcocks; Lombard loved to tease him, and he loved her to do it to him. It was during this time (1941) that he made his infamous comment "Actors are cattle," which the press seized on and he never shook loose. Lombard added her opinion to his remark by going out and buying three calves, having a corral built, and labeling each with three stars' names: Carole Lombard, Robert Montgomery, and Gene Raymond. He loved it! He parried by making her read her lines off a chalkboard, which completely threw her. She got back at him by directing his cameo appearance in the film, insisting on take after take, just for the fun of it. Hitchcock was as wounded as anyone could be at her untimely loss.

He made an attempt to cast another blonde type in *Saboteur,* but Priscilla Lane was too earthy for his needs. Teresa Wright was perfect in his following film, *Shadow of a Doubt,* but she was not a blonde. Then he did *Lifeboat,* with the most unique of the Hitchcock sirens.

Tallulah Bankhead amused Hitchcock with her unexpected attitudes,

Tallulah Bankhead was an unusual Hitchcock heroine with whom he got along famously.
(The Museum of Modern Art/Film Stills Archive)

Ingrid Bergman was one of the classic Hitchcock blondes. A close personal friend, he is seen with her in this early publicity shot. (Memory Shop)

such as her dislike for Walter Slezak, whom she referred to as "That Nazi." In Taylor's biography of Hitchcock, he recounts a most bemusing problem that arose with his eccentric female star. Bankhead adamantly eschewed wearing underwear and saw no reason to change her ways just because she had to climb a ladder every day to get into the tank where *Lifeboat* was being filmed. This daily ritual began to attract larger and larger throngs of technicians and bystanders. Eventually this got back to Darryl Zanuck, the executive producer of the studio where the film was being made. He asked Hitchcock if he could do something about it, to which Hitchcock replied, "Willingly. Of course it will have to go through the proper channels, and I don't know which to go through—makeup, wardrobe, or hairdressing!"

After *Lifeboat* Hitchcock found his first "true blonde," the talented Ingrid Bergman. He cast her in his next two films, *Spellbound* and *Notorious,* and again in 1949 in *Under Capricorn.* He found her to be wonderfully intelligent, capable of projecting his idea of surface cool melting into emotional fire. They became close friends, even after the incident on the set of *Under Capricorn.*

Stage Fright followed. Marlene Dietrich was well suited to her role and became a good personal friend. She and Hitchcock would often go art shopping together, as he respected her good taste, and she his. She found him to be very professional and easy to work with because he knew precisely what he wanted to achieve on the set.

Whatever disappointment *Strangers on a Train* and *I Confess* brought him in terms of actresses faded with *Dial M for Murder* and the appearance of Grace Kelly. She worked

Marlene Dietrich was perfect in Stage Fright *and helped Hitchcock with his personal art collection.* (The Museum of Modern Art/ Film Stills Archive)

Patricia Hitchcock appeared in Stage Fright. *This aspiring actress would soon marry and give Hitchcock three granddaughters.* (The Museum of Modern Art/Film Stills Archive)

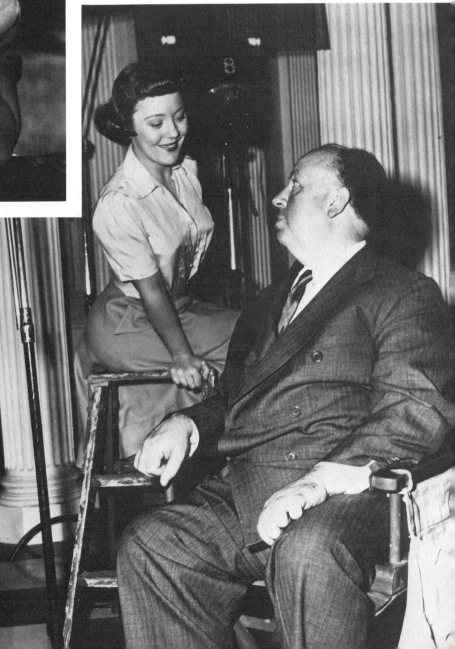

with Hitchcock in a succession of films: *Dial M for Murder, Rear Window,* and *To Catch a Thief.* With Kelly, Hitchcock found the personification of his blonde ideal: a beautiful, seemingly detached blonde, capable of anything. She never objected to his advice on how to dress, eat, and walk. In fact, Hitchcock is probably responsible for her next career, as he introduced her to Prince Rainier.

He expounded on this idea of cultivating screen personalities in an interview in 1956 with *Cosmopolitan.* Using Grace Kelly as an example, he said, "I really fix them up. She was rather mousy in *High Noon,* but she blossomed out for me in her next two films." He went on to explain that in order for there to be a sexual quality on the screen, the actress must have a mysterious element. "This requires showing her as an enigmatic person who might appear in a taxicab with a man who does not know whether she will shrink into a corner or tear off his clothes." He made it very clear how this was accomplished. "My technique goes like this: If an actress is drab, I set her on fire with sequins. If she is a sexy number to start with, I soft-pedal her. I cover her up at the start and bring her out by easy stages. Now, Marilyn Monroe, for instance. If I ever have her for a picture, I'll start her out as a nun!"

His next find was Vera Miles, whom he used in *The Wrong Man* and *Psycho.* He was moved by her performance in *The Wrong Man* and thought perhaps she was proficient enough as an actress to develop the sophisticated demeanor he enjoyed—but he never had a chance to find out. She became pregnant before *Vertigo* went before the camera, and Hitchcock's disappointment was great.

Doris Day was a blonde, but not a Hitchcock blonde. However, she did give a fine performance in the remake of The Man Who Knew Too Much. (Memory Shop)

Eva Marie Saint was probably the last of his blonde heroines, giving a sultry but subdued performance in *North by Northwest.* He regretted they were not able to work together again. She was appreciative of his guidance and he did much to broaden her appeal as a performer. Then along came what he thought would be his next Grace Kelly. While watching a television commercial he spotted a model named Tippi Hedren.

Tippi Hedren was placed under personal contract and cast in *The Birds.* At first she was responsive to his help, but sadly, she was just not an accomplished actress. Her reviews for *The Birds* were not good, and whether or not Hitchcock agreed is not known.

Grace Kelly was the perfect Hitchcock blonde—a fragile yet fiery actress of exquisite beauty. (Memory Shop)

For Vertigo, *Hitchcock wanted Vera Miles, but she became pregnant and he cast Kim Novak. The critics liked her but he has said that as an actress "she was only an adequacy."* (Memory Shop)

Eva Marie Saint as she appeared in North by Northwest. *He thought her excellent in* On the Waterfront *and wanted to bring out her sexual qualities. He succeeded with Cary Grant playing her lover in this scene from the film.* (Memory Shop)

But since she was under full contract he decided to use her in *Marnie.* It was during the filming of that picture that the impossible happened— Hitchcock lost his temper on the set. It occurred when Hedren asked to go off for a day or two and he refused. Words were exchanged, and he left the set angry and bitter over her unforgivable indiscretion—she had referred to his weight! After that unfortunate incident, he never again tried to find his cool blonde, but cast his remaining films according to the requirements of the part.

Hitchcock's relationship with his wife, Alma, was a private matter, but it is well known that she was his best critic and often more involved in the films than many realize. She began as his assistant director and went on to do the script adaptations for six of his films. She wrote or collaborated on ten of his screenplays. She was never fond of publicity and left the high-profile work to him, content to run the show from backstage.

Hitchcock enjoyed talking about her, though, and often took the opportunity to relate his marriage proposal to her. "The day I proposed marriage to Alma she was lying in an upper bunk of a ship's cabin. The ship was floundering in a most desperate way and so was Alma, who was seasick. I couldn't risk being flowery for fear that in her wretched state she would think I was discussing a movie script. As it was, she groaned, nodded her head,

The Hitchcocks loved to travel, often visiting
locations for their films. They worked as a team—
she being his best and most particular critic.
As a trained film editor who grew up in the business,
she generally eschewed publicity, leaving that to
her husband. (Memory Shop)

Mrs. Hitchcock, Alma Reville, was the most important Hitchcock heroine. She helped script or adapt over fifteen films. Here she works with close Hitchcock assistant, Joan Harrison, on the Suspicion *script in 1941.* (The Museum of Modern Art/Film Stills Archive)

and burped. It was one of my greatest scenes—a little weak on dialogue, perhaps, but beautifully staged and not overplayed."

They made for an unusual Hollywood couple, living as they did in the same house in Bel Air throughout their marriage. She did the cooking and employed only a cleaning lady to help with household chores. One extravagance in their home was a huge eat-in kitchen, with a walk-in freezer and complete wine cellar. Most important, they made movies together, which was probably the best thing of all.

Alma seemed to understand her husband's many habits. For example, he was compulsive about keeping a neat desk and wouldn't drive a car for fear of arrest, so Alma did the driving. (Memory Shop)

"A few years ago, in Santa Rosa, California, I caught a side view of myself in a store window and screamed with fright. Since then I limit myself to a three-course dinner of appetizer, fish, and meat, with only one bottle of vintage wine with each course." —*Hitchcock*

Hitchcock, by his own admission, was an unattractive man. He was overweight and went on and off various diets. He always knew that his living would be made with his mind and never had any delusions about it not being that way. However, he would become, through his own devices, one of the world's most easily recognizable public figures. Through various methods of public relations, he nurtured a universal public image. One of the most successful of these devices was his often split-second appearance in cameo in many of his theatrical films.

His critics, and especially other directors, have wondered how a man of his ability and artistic stature would make these obviously publicity-related appearances. To understand this peculiar phenomenon, it is helpful to go back to his early days in the silents.

In the summer 1980 edition of *Sight and Sound,* the British film quarterly, Ivor Montagu commented about Hitchcock's notions on this question. At this time, Hitchcock attended a regular meeting of fellow filmmakers called "the Hate Club." These aspiring British silent film directors and producers gathered together to let off steam about the industry. At one of these functions, the question of who they made their films for arose. Hitchcock skipped over "the public" and "the boss" as being too simple an answer. Someone else suggested "the distributor," arguing that unless they liked it, it might not get shown. Hitchcock went further. He contended that "the press" was the main audience. His reasoning was simple: If you make yourself known publicly as a director, if you are mentioned in the press in connection with your work, then you will have the power to do whichever film you wanted.

His method for getting this sort of attention was to create unusual camera work that would gain attention and to make a personal appearance in each film. The latter became more successful then he ever dreamed, and his public continues to think of him in terms of these little cameos. They remained a part of the Hitchcock legacy.

A common misconception is that Hitchcock appears in every one of his fifty-three films. In fact, he is only in thirty-six of them. As many of these shots as possible are presented here.

The film cameos went hand in hand with his public appearances, interviews, and the introductions he did on his television show. He was uncomfortable with live speeches or lectures, but often enjoyed them once he got over his initial stage fright. That he could be so publicly aware and still maintain his creative dignity was much to his credit.

Many have asked if Hitchcock was a *nice* man. He was a polite man, an honest man, and a private man. He could be formidable and manipulative and he was, after all, highly competitive. Ray Bradbury remembers him as somewhat formal and cool to his employees, but with a certain amiability. He preferred his employees to wear a jacket and tie on his set, which was always quiet and organized. He expected everyone to know his or her job, and for this reason he never looked through the camera, for example, as he already knew what was supposed to be there.

He had his dark side. He was fond of referring to his audience as "the moron masses," a phrase he also applied to extras. He enjoyed making outrageous remarks, but they always rang with a touch of the truth. Bradbury was with him on location for *Family Plot,* and as the tour busses rumbled by with shouts of "Hi, Alfie," his whispered remarks, while he smiled and waved, are not printable.

He called himself "a poet of civilized suspense." He said, "I aim to provide the public with beneficial shocks. Civilization has become so protective that we're no longer able to get our goose bumps instinctively. The only way to remove the numbness and revive our moral equilibrium is to use artificial means to bring about the shock. The best way to achieve that, it seems to me, is through a movie."

Ernest Lehman, in his eloquent eulogy in *American Film* magazine, tells us what he did so well. "To the very end, he never stopped wanting to delight us, to manipulate us and excite us and tantalize us and move us and fascinate us and enthrall us and fill us with dread and laughter and curiosity. He was a mischievous child clothed in the black serge garb of a world-weary sophisticate, and he took marvelous enjoyment in playing his games and letting us watch.

"How rewarding it has been, how reassuring practically all of all our lives, to have been in the lap, in the hands, under the spell, of this giant, this genius, this gentle man. And now, this morning, he pauses . . .

"Hitch . . . what happens next?"

Hitchcock's cameos began when he needed extras and couldn't afford them, such as sitting with his back to the camera in The Lodger. *He also appears at the end of the film in a crowd scene.* (The Rank Organization Limited)

In Blackmail, *he made his first noticeable appearance. Soon he will take offense at the young stranger and swat him with his hat.* (EMI Films Limited)

He often appeared passing along the street, as in Murder. (EMI Films Limited)

He believed a director worked for the press and should therefore try to stay noticed. Here he films his appearance in Sabotage. (The Rank Organization Limited)

PRICES
OF
ADMISSION

Balcony......

Stalls {Front
Last Two
Rows

In Young and Innocent *he donned a hat and played a bumbling photographer.* (The Rank Organization Limited)

After a time he became bored with his appearances, feeling that they distracted the audience from the plot, but he continued to make them. This one is taken from The Lady Vanishes. (The Rank Organization Limited)

Some cameos are more noticeable than others, such as this one in Rebecca *with George Sanders.* (The Museum of Modern Art/Film Stills Archive)

In Foreign Correspondent *he passed Joel McCrea reading a newspaper.* (The Museum of Modern Art/ Film Stills Archive)

How to appear in a movie with a single set and no extras? In a newspaper, of course, held by William Bendix in Lifeboat. (The Museum of Modern Art/Film Stills Archive)

146

He favored cigars in many of his appearances, such as this one from Spellbound. (The Museum of Modern Art/ Film Stills Archive)

An unobtrusive party guest sips champagne in Notorious. (The Museum of Modern Art/Film Stills Archive)

He had a fondness for cellos in The Paradine Case.
(The Museum of Modern Art/Film Stills Archive)

His only costume appearance was in Jamaica Inn.
He appeared twice in this film. (The British Film
Institute/National Film Archive/Stills Library)

He passes, then turns to look back at Jane Wyman in Stage Fright. (The Museum of Modern Art/ Film Stills Archive)

This time a double bass served as his prop in Strangers on a Train. (The Museum of Modern Art/Film Stills Archive)

For I Confess, *he appeared in the distance at the beginning of the movie.* (The Museum of Modern Art/Film Stills Archive)

One of his subtler cameos occurs in Dial M for Murder. *He is in the photograph held by Ray Milland.* (The Museum of Modern Art/Film Stills Archive)

Another street appearance in Vertigo.
(The Museum of Modern Art/
Film Stills Archive)

He didn't want to slow the plot of
North by Northwest, *so he appears during
the credits, missing a bus.* (The Museum
of Modern Art/Film Stills Archive)

In The Birds *he passes Tippi Hedren.
The dogs are his own prize
Sealyham terriers, Stanley and
Geoffrey.* (Memory Shop)

For Torn Curtain, *he appeared in a hotel lobby with a soggy infant on his lap.*
(The Museum of Modern Art/Film Stills Archive)

Topaz *catches Hitchcock in a wheelchair. He must*
have felt that he deserved a rest. (The British Film
Institute/National Film Archive/Stills Library)

Hitchcock's last cameo appearance was in Family Plot. *As you can see, he needs* two *death certificates from the registrar's office.* (The British Film Institute/National Film Archive/ Stills Library)

Hitchcock and Alma—a durable if unusual team
by Hollywood standards. They never cared
much for the Hollywood high life, only for each
other and their profession. They were a
perfect team. (The British Film Institute/National Film
Archive/Stills Library)

The Hitchcock legacy lives on in festivals,
retrospectives, television, and the movie
theaters throughout the world. It is a remarkable
achievement for a remarkable talent.
(The Museum of Modern Art/Film Stills Archive)

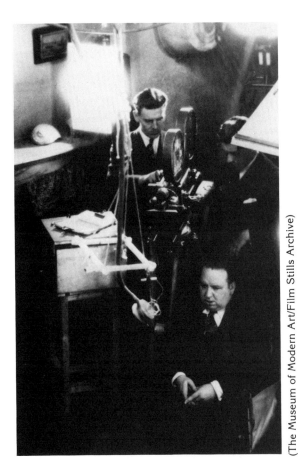

Filmography

The Silent Films

THE PLEASURE GARDEN / 1925
Production: Michael Balcon (Gainsborough), Eric Pommer (Emelka-G.B.A.); *Screenplay:* Eliot Stannard, from the novel by Oliver Sandys; *Director of Photography:* Baron Ventigmilia; *Assistant Director:* Alma Reville; *Studio:* Emelka, at Munich; *Distributors:* Wardour & F.; USA, Amyon Independent; *Principal Actors:* Virginia Valli (Patsy Brand), Carmelita Geraghty (Jill Cheyne), Miles Mander (Levet), John Stuart (Hugh Fielding), Frederic K. Martini, Florence Helminger, George Snell, C. Falkenburg.

THE MOUNTAIN EAGLE / 1926
Production: Gainsborough, Emelka; *Producer:* Michael Balcon; *Screenplay:* Eliot Stannard; *Director of Photography:* Baron Ventigmilia; *Studio:* Emelka, at Munich; *Location Work:* Austrian Tyrol; *Distributors:* Wardour & F.; USA, Artlee; Independent Distributors; *Principal*

Actors: Bernard Boetzke (Pettigrew), Nita Naldi (Beatrice), Malcolm Keen (Fear o'God), John Hamilton (Edward Pettigrew).

THE LODGER (A Story of the London Fog) / 1926
Production: Gainsborough, Michael Balcon; *Screenplay:* Alfred Hitchcock and Eliot Stannard, from the novel by Mrs. Belloc-Lowndes; *Director of Photography:* Baron Ventigmilia; *Sets:* C. Wilfred Arnold and Bertram Evans; *Editing and Subtitles:* Ivor Montagu; *Assistant Director:* Alma Reville; *Studio:* Islington; *Distributor:* Wardour & F.; *Principal Actors:* Ivor Novello (the lodger), June (Daisy Jackson), Marie Ault (Mrs. Jackson), Arthur Chesney (Mr. Jackson), Malcolm Keen (Joe Betts).

DOWNHILL / 1927
Production: Michael Balcon, Gainsborough, G.B.; *Screenplay:* Eliot Stannard, from the play by Ivor Novello and Constance Collier, written under the pseudonym David Lestrange; *Director of Photography:* Claude McDonnell; *Editing:* Ivor Montagu; *Studio:* Islington; *Distributors:* Wardour & F.; USA, World Wide Distributors; *Principal Actors:* Ivor Novello (Roddy Berwick), Ben Webster (Doctor Dowson), Robin Irvine (Tim Wakely), Sybil Rhoda (Sybil Wakely), Lillian Braithwaite (Lady Berwick), and Hannah Jones, Violet Farebrother, Isabel Jeans, Norman McKinne, Jerrold Robertshaw, Annette Benson, Ian Hunter, Barbara Gott, Alfred Goddard.

EASY VIRTUE / 1927
Production: Michael Balcon, Gainsborough Production; *Screenplay:* Eliot Stannard, from the play by Noel Coward; *Director of Photography:* Claude McDonnell: *Editing:* Ivor Montagu; *Studio:* Islington; *Distributors:* Wardour & F.; USA, World Wide Distributors; *Principal Actors:* Isabel Jeans (Larita Filton), Franklin Byall (M. Filton), Eric Bransby Williams (the correspondent), Ian Hunter (plaintiff's counsel), Robin Irvine (John Whittaker), Violet Farebrother (Mrs. Whittaker), and Frank Elliot, Darcia Deane, Dorothy Boyd, Enid Stamp-Taylor.

THE RING / 1927
Production: British International Pictures, G.B.; *Producer:* John Maxwell; *Screenplay:* Alfred Hitchcock; *Adaptation:* Alma Reville; *Director of Photography:* Jack Cox; *Assistant Director:* Frank Mills; *Studio:* Elstree; *Distributors:* Wardour & F.; *Principal Actors:* Carl Brisson (Jack Sander), Lillian Hall-Davies (Nelly), Ian Hunter (Bob Corby), Forrester Harvey (Harry), and Harry Terry, Gordon Harker, Billy Wells.

THE FARMER'S WIFE / 1928
Production: British International Pictures, G.B., *Producer:* John Maxwell; *Screenplay:* Alfred Hitchcock, from the play by Eden Philpotts; *Director of Photography:* Jack Cox; *Assistant Director:*

Frank Mills; *Editing:* Alfred Booth; *Studio:* Elstree; *Location Work:* Wales; *Distributors:* Wardour & F.; *Principal Actors:* James Thomas (Samuel Sweetland), Maud Gill (Thirza Tapper), Gordon Harker (Cheirdles Ash), and Louise Pounds, Olga Slade, Antonia Brough.

CHAMPAGNE / 1928
Production: British International Pictures, G.B.; *Screenplay:* Eliot Stannard; *Director of Photography:* Jack Cox; *Studio:* Elstree; *Distributor:* Wardour & F.; *Principal Actors:* Betty Balfour (Betty), Gordon Harker (her father), Ferdinand Von Alten (the passenger), Jean Bradin (the young man), and Jack Trevor, Marcel Vibert.

THE MANXMAN / 1929
Production: British International Pictures, G.B.; *Producer:* John Maxwell; *Screenplay:* Eliot Stannard, from the novel by Sir Hall Caine; *Director of Photography:* Jack Cox; *Assistant Director:* Frank Mills; *Studio:* Elstree; *Distributors:* Wardour & F.; *USA,* Ufa Eastman Division; *Principal Actors:* Carl Brisson (Pete), Malcolm Keen (Philip), Anny Ondra (Kate), Randle Ayrton (her father), and Clare Greet.

The Sound Films

BLACKMAIL / 1929
Production: British International Pictures, G.B.; *Producer:* John Maxwell; *Screenplay:* Alfred Hitchcock, Benn W. Levy, and Charles Bennett, from the play by Charles Bennett; *Adaptation:* Alfred Hitchcock; *Dialogue:* Benn W. Levy; *Director of Photography:* Jack Cox; *Sets:* Wilfred C. Arnold and Norman Arnold; *Music:* Campbell and Connely, finished and arranged by Hubert Bath and Henry Stafford, performed by the British Symphony Orchestra under the direction of John Reynders; *Editing:* Emile de Ruelle; *Studio:* Elstree; *Distributors:* Wardour & F.; *USA,* Sono Art World Wide Pictures; *Principal Actors:* Anny Ondra (Alice White), Sara Allgood (Mrs. White), John Longden (Frank Webber), Charles Paton (Mr. White), Donald Calthrop (Tracy), Cyril Ritchard (the artist), and Harvey Braban, Hannah Jones, Phyllis Monkman, ex-detective Sergeant Bishop.

JUNO AND THE PAYCOCK / 1929
Production: British International Pictures; *Producer:* John Maxwell; *Screenplay:* Alfred Hitchcock and Alma Reville, from the play by Sean O'Casey; *Director of Photography:* Jack Cox; *Sets:* Norman Arnold; *Editing:* Emile de Reulle; *Studio:* Elstree; *Distributors:* Wardour & F.; *USA,* British International by Capt. Harold Auten; *Principal Actors:* Sara Allgood (Juno), Edward Chapman (Captain Boyle), Sidney Morgan (Joxer), Marie

O'Neill (Mrs. Madigan), and John Laurie, Dennis Wyndham, John Longden, Kathleen O'Regan, Dave Morris, Fred Schwartz.

MURDER / 1929
Production: British International Pictures, G.B.; *Producer:* John Maxwell; *Screenplay:* Alma Reville, from the work by Clemence Dane (pseudonym of Winifred Ashton) and Helen Simpson, *Enter Sir John; Adaptation:* Alfred Hitchcock and Walter Mycroft; *Director of Photography:* Jack Cox; *Sets:* John Mead; *Editing:* René Harrison; *Supervision:* Emile de Ruelle; *Studio:* Elstree; *Distributor:* Wardour & F.; *Principal Actors:* Herbert Marshall (Sir John Menier), Nora Baring (Diana Baring), Phyllis Konstam (Dulcie Markham), Edward Chapman (Ted Markham), Miles Mander (Gordon Druce), Esme Percy (Handel Fane), Donald Calthrop (Ion Stewart), and Amy Brandon Thomas, Joynson Powell, Esme V. Chaplin, Marie Wright, S. J. Warmington, Hannah Jones, R. E. Jeffrey, Alan Stainer, Kenneth Kove, Guy Pelham, Matthew Boulton, Violet Farebrother, Ross Jefferson, Clare Greet, Drusilla Vills, Robert Easton, William Fazan, George Smythson.

THE SKIN GAME / 1931
Production: British International Pictures, G.B.; *Producer:* John Maxwell; *Screenplay:* Alfred Hitchcock and Alma Reville, from the play by John Galsworthy; *Additional Dialogues:* Alma Reville; *Director of Photography:* Jack Cox, assisted by Charles Martin; *Editing:* René Harrison and A. Gobett; *Studio:* Elstree; *Distributors:* Wardour & F.; *USA,* British International; *Principal Actors:* Edmund Gwenn (Mr. Hornblower), Jill Esmond (Jill), John Longden (Charles), C. V. France (Mr. Hillcrest), Helen Haye (Mrs. Hillcrest), Phyllis Konstam (Chloe), Frank Lawton (Rolfe), and Herbert Ross, Dora Gregory, Edward Chapman, R. E. Jeffrey, George Bancroft, Ronald Frankau.

RICH AND STRANGE / 1932
Production: British International Pictures, G.B.; *Producer:* John Maxwell; *Screenplay:* Alma Reville and Val Valentine, from a theme by Dale Collins; *Adaptation:* Alfred Hitchcock; *Directors of Photography:* Jack Cox and Charles Martin; *Sets:* C. Wilfred Arnold; *Music:* Hal Dolphe, directed by John Reynders; *Editing:* Winifred Cooper and René Harrison; *Sound Engineer:* Alec Murray; *Studio:* Elstree; *Location Work:* Marseilles, Port Said, Colombo, Suez; *Distributors:* Wardour & F.; *USA,* Powers Pictures; *Principal Actors:* Henry Kendall (Freddy Hill), Joan Barry (Emily Hill), Betty Amann (The Princess), Percy Marmont (Gordon), Elsie Randolph (the old lady).

NUMBER SEVENTEEN / 1932
Production: British International Pictures, G.B.; *Producer:* John Maxwell; *Screenplay:* Alfred

Hitchcock, from the play and the novel by Jefferson Farjeon; *Director of Photography:* Jack Cox; *Studio:* Elstree; *Distributor:* Wardour & F.; *Principal Actors:* Léon M. Lion (Ben), Anne Grey (the young girl), John Stuart (the detective), and Donald Calthrop, Barry Jones, Garry Marsh.

WALTZES FROM VIENNA / 1933
Production: Gaumont-British, G.F.D., G.B.; *Screenplay:* Alma Reville and Guy Bolton, from the play by Guy Bolton; *Sets:* Alfred Junge and Peter Proud; *Music:* Johann Strauss the Elder and Johann Strauss the Younger; *Studio:* Lime Grove; *Distributors:* G.F.D.; USA, Tom Arnold; *Principal Actors:* Jessie Matthews (Rasi), Esmond Knight (Shani Strauss), Frank Vosper (the prince), Fay Compton (the countess), Edmund Gwenn (Johann Strauss the Elder), Robert Hale (Ebezeder), Hindle Edgar (Leopold), Marcus Barron (Drexter), Charles Heslop, Sybil Grove, Billy Shine, Junior, Bertram Dench, B. M. Lewis, Cyril Smith, Betty Huntley Wright, Berinoff and Charlot.

THE MAN WHO KNEW TOO MUCH / 1934
Production: Gaumont-British Pictures, G.B.; *Producer:* Michael Balcon; *Associate Producer:* Ivor Montagu; *Screenplay:* A. R. Rawlinson, Charles Bennett, D. B. Wyndham Lewis, Edwin Greenwood, from an original theme by Charles Bennett and D. B. Wyndham Lewis; *Additional Dialogue:* Emlyn Williams; *Director of Photography:* Curt Courant; *Sets:* Alfred Junge and Peter Proud; *Music:* Arthur Benjamin, directed by Louis Levy; *Editing:* H. St.C. Stewart; *Studio:* Lime Grove; *Distributors:* G.F.D.; *Principal Actors:* Leslie Banks (Bob Lawrence), Edna Best (Jill Lawrence), Peter Lorre (Abbot), Frank Vosper (Ramon Levine), Hugh Wakefield (Clive), Nova Pilbeam (Betty Lawrence), Pierre Fresnay (Louis Bernard), and Cicely Oates, D. A. Clarke Smith, George Curzon.

THE 39 STEPS / 1935
Production: Gaumont-British; *Producer:* Michael Balcon; *Associate Producer:* Ivor Montagu; *Screenplay and Adaptation:* Charles Bennett and Alma Reville, from the novel by John Buchan; *Additional Dialogue:* Ian Hay; *Director of Photography:* Bernard Knowles; *Sets:* Otto Werndorff and Albert Jullion; *Costumes:* J. Strassner; *Music:* Louis Levy; *Editing:* Derek N. Twist; *Sound Engineer:* A. Birch, Full Range Recording System at Shepherd's Bush, London; *Studio:* Lime Grove; *Distributors:* G.F.D.; *Principal Actors:* Madeleine Carroll (Pamela), Robert Donat (Richard Hannay), Lucie Mannheim (Miss Smith-Annabella), Godfrey Tearle (Professor Jordan), Peggy Ashcroft (Mrs. Crofter), John Laurie (Crofter, the farmer), Helen Haye (Mrs. Jordan), Frank Cellier (the sheriff), Wylie Watson (Memory).

SECRET AGENT / 1936
Production: Gaumont-British; *Producers:* Michael Balcon and Ivor Montagu; *Screenplay:* Charles Bennett, from the play by Campbell Dixon, adapted from the novel *Ashenden* by Somerset Maugham; *Adaptation:* Alma Reville; *Dialogues:* Ian Hay and Jesse Lasky, Jr.; *Director of Photography:* Bernard Knowles; *Sets:* Otto Werndorff and Albert Jullion; *Costumes:* J. Strasser; *Music:* Louis Levy; *Editing:* Charles Frend; *Studio:* Lime Grove; *Distributors:* G.F.D.; USA, G.B. Production; *Principal Actors:* Madeleine Carroll (Elsa Carrington), John Gielgud (Richard Ashenden), Peter Lorre (the general), Robert Young (Robert Marvin), and Percy Marmont, Florence Kahn, Lilli Palmer, Charles Carson, Michael Redgrave.

SABOTAGE / 1936
Production: Shepherd, Gaumont-British Pictures; *Producers:* Michael Balcon and Ivor Mantagu; *Screenplay:* Charles Bennett, from the novel *The Secret Agent* by Joseph Conrad; *Adaptation:* Alma Reville; *Dialogues:* Ian Hay, Helen Simpson, and E. V. H. Emmett; *Director of Photography:* Bernard Knowles; *Sets:* Otto Werndorff and Albert Jullion; *Music:* Louis Levy; *Costumes:* J. Strassner; *Editing:* Charles Frend; *Studio:* Lime Grove; *Cartoon:* Sequence of "Who Killed Cock Robin?" a Silly Symphony of Walt Disney, used with his permission; *Distributors:* G.F.D.; USA, G.B. Productions; *Principal Actors:* Sylvia Sidney (Sylvia Verloc), Oscar Homolka (Verloc, her husband), Desmond Tester (Sylvia's brother), John Loder (Ted, the Detective), Joyce Barbour (Renee), Matthew Boulton (The Superintendent), and S. J. Barmington, William Dewherst, Peter Bull, Torin Thatcher, Austin Trevor, Clare Greet, Sam Wilkinson, Sara Allgood, Martita Hunt, Pamela Bevan.

YOUNG AND INNOCENT / 1937
Production: Gainsborough, Gaumont-British; *Producer:* Edward Black; *Screenplay:* Charles Bennett and Alma Reville, from the novel *A Shilling For Candles* by Josephine Tey; *Director of Photography:* Bernard Knowles; *Sets:* Alfred Junge; *Music:* Louis Levy; *Editing:* Charles Frend; *Studios:* Lime Grove and Pinewood; *Distributors:* G.F.D.; USA, G.B. Production; *Principal Actors:* Derrick de Marney (Robert Tisdall), Nova Pilbeam (Erica), Percy Marmont (Colonel Burgoyne), Edward Rigby (Old Will), Mary Clare (Erica's aunt), John Longden (Kent), George Curzon (Guy), Basil Radford (Uncle Basil), and Pamela Carme, George Merritt, J. H. Roberts, Jerry Verno, H. F. Maltby, John Miller, Torin Thatcher, Peggy Simpson, Anna Konstam, Beatrice Varley, William Fazan, Frank Atkinson, Fred O'Donovan, Albert Chevalier, Richard George, Jack Vyvian, Clive Baxter, Pamela Bevan, Humberston Wright, Gerry Fitzgerald, Syd Crossley.

THE LADY VANISHES / 1938
Production: Gainsborough Pictures, G.B.;
Producer: Edward Black; *Screenplay:* Sidney
Gilliat and Frank Launder, from the novel *The
Wheel Spins* by Ethel Lina White; *Adaptation:*
Alma Reville; *Director of Photography:* Jack
Cox; *Sets:* Alex Vetchinsky, Maurice Cater, and
Albert Jullion; *Music:* Louis Levy; *Editing:* Alfred
Roome and R. E. Dearing; *Studio:* Lime Grove;
Sound Engineer: Sidney Wiles; *Distributors:*
G.B.; USA, G.B. Production; *Principal Actors:*
Margaret Lockwood (Iris Henderson), Michael
Redgrave (Gilbert), Paul Lukas (Dr. Hartz), Dame
May Whitty (Miss Froy), Googie Withers (Blanche),
Cecil Parker (Mr. Todhunter), Linden Travers
(Mrs. Todhunter), Lary Clare (the baroness),
Naunton Wayne (Caldicott), Basil Radford
(Charters), and Emil Borco, Zelma Vas Dias,
Phillipe Leaver, Sally Stewart, Catherine Lacey,
Josephine Wilson, Charles Oliver, Kathleen
Tremaine.

JAMAICA INN / 1939
Production: Mayflowers Productions, G.B.;
Producers: Erich Pommer and Charles Laughton;
Production Manager: Hugh Perceval; *Screenplay:*
Sydney Gilliat and John Harrison, from the novel
by Daphne du Maurier; *Dialogues:* Sydney Gilliat
and J. B. Priestley; *Adaptation:* Alma Reville;
Directors of Photography: Harry Stradling and
Bernard Knowles; *Special Effects:* Harry Watt;
Sets: Tom N. Moraham; *Costumes:* Molly
McArthur; *Music:* Eric Fenby, directed by
Frederic Lewis; *Editing:* Robert Hamer; *Sound
Engineer:* Jack Rogerson; *Distributors:* Associated
British; USA, Paramount; *Principal Actors:*
Charles Laughton (Sir Humphrey Pengaltan),
Horace Hodges (Chadwick, his butler), Hay Petrie
(his groom), Frederick Piper (his broker), Leslie
Banks (Joss Merlyn), Marie Ney (Patience, his
wife), Maureen O'Hara (Mary, his niece), and
Robert Newton, Herbert Lomas, Clare Greet,
William Delvin, Mabel Terry Lewis, George Curzon,
Basil Radford, Emlyn Williams, Roy Frumkes,
Wylie Watson, Morland Graham, Edwin Green-
wood, Stephan Haggard, Mervyn Johns.

REBECCA / 1940
Production: David O. Selznick, USA; *Producer:*
David O. Selznick; *Screenplay:* Robert E. Sherwood
and Joan Harrison, from the novel by Daphne
du Maurier; *Adaptation:* Philip MacDonald and
Michael Hogan; *Director of Photography:* George
Barnes; *Sets:* Lyle Wheeler; *Music:* Franz Waxman;
Editing: Hal C. Kern; *Studio:* Selznick International;
Distributor: United Artists; *Principal Actors:*
Laurence Olivier (Maxim de Winter), Joan
Fontaine (Mrs. de Winter), George Sanders (Jack
Favell), Judith Anderson (Mrs. Danvers), Nigel
Bruce (Major Giles Lacey), C. Aubrey Smith
(Colonel Julyan), and Reginald Denny, Gladys

Cooper, Philip Winter, Edward Fielding, Florence
Bates, Leo G. Carroll, Forrester Harvey, Lumsden
Hare, Leonard Carey, Edith Sharpe, Melville
Cooper.

FOREIGN CORRESPONDENT / 1940
Production: Walter Wanger, United Artists;
Screenplay: Charles Bennett and Joan Harrison;
Dialogues: James Hilton and Robert Benchley;
Director of Photography: Rudolph Mate; *Special
Effects:* Lee Zavitz; *Sets:* William Cameron Menzies
and Alexander Golitzen; *Music:* Alfred Newman;
Editing: Otto Lovering and Dorothy Spencer;
Assistant Director: Edmond Bernoudy; *Studio:*
United Artists at Hollywood; *Distributor:* United
Artists; *Principal Actors:* Joel McCrea (Johnny
Jones), Laraine Day (Carol Fisher), Herbert
Marshall (Stephen Fisher), George Sanders
(Herbert Foliott), Albert Bassermann (Van Meer),
Robert Benchley (Stebbins), Eduardo Cianelli
(Krug), Edmund Gwenn (Rowley), Harry Davenport
(Mr. Powers), and Martin Losleck, Eddie Conrad,
Gertrude W. Hoffman, Jane Novak, Ken Christy,
Crawford Kent, Joan Brodel-Leslie, Louis Borell.

MR. AND MRS. SMITH / 1941
Production: RKO; *Executive Producer:* Harry E.
Edington; *Story and Screenplay:* Norman Krasna;
Director of Photography: Harry Stradling, ASC;
Sets: Van Nest Polglase and L. P. Williams;
Music: Roy Webb; *Special Effects:* Vernon L.
Walker; *Editing:* William Hamilton; *Studio:* RKO;
Distributor: RKO; *Principal Actors:* Carole Lombard
(Ann Smith and Ann Kransheimer), Robert
Montgomery (David Smith), Gene Raymond
(Jeff Custer), Jack Carson (Chuck Benson), Philip
Merivale (Mr. Custer), Lucille Watson (Mrs. Custer),
William Tracy (Sammy), and Charles Halton,
Esther Dale, Emma Dunn, Betty Compson,
Patricia Farr, William Edmunds, Adela Pearce,
Murray Alper, D. Johnson, James Flavin, Sam
Harris.

SUSPICION / 1941
Production: RKO; *Screenplay:* Samson Raphaelson,
Joan Harrison, and Alma Reville, from the novel
Before the Fact by Francis Iles (Anthony Berkeley);
Director of Photography: Harry Stradling, ASC;
Special Effects: Vernon L. Walker; *Sets:* Van Nest
Polglase; *Assistant:* Carroll Clark; *Music:* Franz
Waxman; *Editing:* William Hamilton; *Sound
Engineer:* John E. Tribly; *Assistant Director:*
Dewey Starkey; *Studio:* RKO; *Distributor:* RKO;
Principal Actors: Cary Grant (John Aysgarth—
"Johnnie"), Joan Fontaine (Lina MacKinlaw), Sir
Cedric Hardwicke (General MacKinlaw), Nigel
Bruce (Beaky), Dame May Whitty (Mrs.
MacKinlaw), Isabel Jeans (Mrs. Newsham), and
Heather Angel, Auriol Lee, Reginald Sheffield,
Leo G. Carroll.

SABOTEUR / 1942
Production: Universal; *Producers:* Frank Lloyd and Jack H. Skirball; *Screenplay:* Petter Viertel, Joan Harrison, and Dorothy Parker, from an original subject by Alfred Hitchcock; *Director of Photography:* Joseph Valentine, ASC; *Sets:* Jack Otterson; *Music:* Charles Previn and Frank Skinner; *Editing:* Otto Ludwig; *Studio:* Universal; *Distributor:* Universal; *Principal Actors:* Robert Cummings (Barry Kane), Priscilla Lane (Patricia Martin), Otto Kruger (Charles Tobin), Alan Baxter (Mr. Freeman), Alma Kruger (Mrs. Van Sutton), and Vaughan Glazer, Dorothy Peterson, Ian Wolfe, Anita Bolster, Jeanne and Lynn Roher, Norman Lloyd, Oliver Blake, Anita Le Deaux, Pedro de Cordoba, Kathryn Adams, Murray Alper, Frances Carson, Billy Curtis.

SHADOW OF A DOUBT / 1943
Production: Universal; *Producer:* Jack H. Skirball; *Screenplay:* Thornton Wilder, Alma Reville, and Sally Benson, from a story by Gordon McDonnell; *Director of Photography:* Joseph Valentine, ASC; *Sets:* John Robinson; *Costumes:* Adrian and Vera West; *Music:* Dimitri Tiomkin, directed by Charles Previn; *Editing:* Milton Carruth; *Studio:* Universal; also shot at Santa Rosa; *Distributor:* Universal; *Principal Actors:* Joseph Cotten (Charlie Oakley, the uncle), Teresa Wright (Charlie Newton), MacDonald Carey (Jack Graham), Patricia Collinge (Emma Newton), Henry Travers (Joseph Newton), Hume Cronyn (Herbie Hawkins), Wallace Ford (Fred Saunders), and Janet Shaw, Estelle Jewell, Eily Malyon, Ethel Griffies, Clarence Muse, Frances Carson, Charlie Bates, Edna May Wonacott.

LIFEBOAT / 1943
Production: Kenneth MacGowan, 20th Century-Fox; *Screenplay:* Jo Swerling, from a story by John Steinbeck; *Director of Photography:* Glen MacWilliams; *Special Effects:* Fred Sersen; *Sets:* James Basevi and Maurice Ransford; *Music:* Hugo Friedhofer, directed by Emil Newman; *Costumes:* Rene Hubert; *Editing:* Dorothy Spencer; *Sound Engineers:* Bernard Fredericks and Roger Heman; *Studio:* 20th Century-Fox; *Distributor:* 20th Century-Fox; *Principal Actors:* Tallulah Bankhead (Constance Porter—"Connie"), William Bendix (Gus Smith), Walter Slezak (Willy, captain of the submarine), Mary Anderson (Alice MacKenzie), John Hodiak (John Kovac), Henry Hull (Charles S. Rittenhouse), Heather Angel (Mrs. Higgins), Hume Cronyn (Stanley Garett), Canada Lee (George Spencer—"Joe," the steward)

SPELLBOUND / 1945
Production: Selznick International; *Producer:* David O. Selznick; *Screenplay:* Ben Hecht, from the novel *The House of Dr. Edwardes* by Francis Beeding (Hilary St. George Saunders and John Palmer); *Adaptation:* Angus McPhail; *Director of*

Photography: George Barnes, ASC; *Special Photographic Effects:* Jack Cosgrove; *Sets:* James Basevi and John Ewing; *Music:* Miklos Rozsa; *Costumes:* Howard Greer; *Editing:* William Ziegler and Hal C. Kern; *Dream Sequence:* Salvador Dali; *Psychiatric Consultant:* May E. Romm; *Studio:* Selznick International; *Distributor:* United Artists; *Principal Actors:* Ingrid Bergman (Doctor Constance Petersen), Gregory Peck (John Ballantine), Jean Acker (the directress), Rhonda Fleming (Mary Carmichel), Donald Curtis (Harry), John Emery (Dr. Fleurot), Leo G. Carroll (Dr. Murchison), Norman Lloyd (Garmes), and Steven Geray, Paul Harvey, Ershine Sandford, Janet Scott, Victor Killian, Bill Goodwin, Art Baker, Wallace Ford, Regis Toomey, Teddy Infuhr, Addison Richards, Dave Willock, George Meader, Matt Morre, Harry Brown, Clarence Straight, Joel Davis, Edward Fielding, Richard Bartell, Michael Chekov.

NOTORIOUS / 1946
Production: Alfred Hitchcock, RKO; *Associate Producer:* Barbara Keon; *Screenplay:* Ben Hecht, from a theme by Alfred Hitchcock; *Director of Photography:* Ted Tetzlaff, ASC; *Special Effects:* Vernon L. Walker and Paul Eagler, ASC; *Sets:* Albert S. D'Agostino, Carrol Clark, Darrell Silvera, and Claude Carpenter; *Costumes:* Edith Head; *Music:* Roy Webb, conducted by Constantin Bakaleinikoff; *Editing:* Theron Warth; *Sound Engineers:* John Tribly and Clem Portman; *Assistant Director:* William Dorfman; *Studio:* RKO; *Distributor:* RKO; *Principal Actors:* Ingrid Bergman (Alicia Huberman), Cary Grant (Devlin), Claude Rains (Alexander Sebastian), Louis Calhern (Paul Prescott), Leopoldine Konstantin (Mrs. Sebastian), Reinhold Schunzel (Dr. Anderson), and Moroni Olsen, Ivan Triesault, Alexis Minotis, Eberhardt Krumschmidt, Fay Baker, Ricardo Costa, Lenore Ulric, Ramon Nomar, Peter von Zerneck, Sir Charles Mandl, Wally Brown.

THE PARADINE CASE / 1947
Production: Selznick International; *Producer:* David O. Selznick; *Screenplay:* David O. Selznick, from the novel by Robert Hichens; *Adaptation:* Alma Reville; *Director of Photography:* Lee Garmes; *Sets:* J. MacMillian Johnson and Thomas Morahan; *Costumes:* Travis Banton; *Music:* Franz Waxman; *Editing:* Hal C. Kern and John Faure; *Studio:* Selznick International; *Distributor:* United Artists; *Principal Actors:* Gregory Peck (Anthony Keane), Anne Todd (Gay Keane), Charles Laughton (Judge Horfield), Ethel Barrymore (Lady Sophie Horfield), Charles Coburn (Sir Simon Flaquer, the lawyer), Louis Jourdan (Andre Latour), Alida Valli (Maddalena, Anna Paradine), and Leo G. Carroll, John Goldsworthy, Isobel Elsom, Lester Matthews, Pat Aherne, Colin Hunter, John Williams.

ROPE / 1948
Production: Transatlantic Pictures, Warner Brothers; *Producers:* Sidney Bernstein and Alfred Hitchcock; *Screenplay:* Arthur Laurents, from the play by Patrick Hamilton; *Adaptation:* Hume Cronyn; *Directors of Photography:* Joseph Valentine and William V. Skall, ASC; *Color:* Technicolor; *Consultant:* Natalie Kalmus; *Sets:* Perry Ferguson; *Music:* Leo F. Forbstein, based on the theme "Perpetual Movement No. 1" by Francis Poulenc; *Costumes:* Adrian; *Editing:* William H. Ziegler; *Studio:* Warner Brothers; *Distributor:* Warner Brothers; *Principal Actors:* James Stewart (Rupert Cadell), John Dall (Shaw Brandon), Joan Chandler (Janet Walker), Sir Cedric Hardwicke (Mr. Kentley, David's father), Constance Collier (Mrs. Atwater), Edith Evanson (Mrs. Wilson, the governess), Douglas Dick (Kenneth Lawrence), Dick Hogan (David Kentley), Farley Granger (Philip).

UNDER CAPRICORN / 1949
Production: Transatlantic Pictures, Warner Brothers, G.B.; *Producers:* Sidney Bernstein and Alfred Hitchcock; *Managing Producers:* John Palmer and Fred Ahern; *Screenplay:* James Bridie, from the novel by Helen Simpson; *Adaptation:* Hume Cronyn; *Director of Photography:* Jack Cardiff, ASC, and Paul Beeson, Ian Craig, David McNeilly, Jack Haste; *Sets:* Tom Morahan; *Music:* Richard Addinsell; conducted by Louis Levy; *Editing:* A. S. Bates; *Costumes:* Roger Furse; *Color:* Technicolor; *Consultants:* Natalie Kalmus and Joan Bridge; *Studio:* MGM, at Elstree; *Distributor:* Warner Brothers; *Principal Actors:* Ingrid Bergman (Lady Henrietta Flusky), Joseph Cotten (Sam Flusky), Michael Wilding (Charles Adare), Margaret Leighton (Milly), Jack Watting (Winter, Flusky's secretary), Cecil Parker (Sir Richard, the tutor), Dennis O'Dea (Corrigan, the attorney general), and Olive Sloan, John Ruddock, Bill Shine, Victor Lucas, Ronald Adam, G. H. Mulcaster, Maureen Delaney, Julia Lang, Betty McDermot, Roderick Lovell, Francis de Wolff.

STAGE FRIGHT / 1950
Production: Alfred Hitchcock, Warner Brothers, G.B.; *Screenplay:* Whitfield Cook, from two stories by Selwyn Jepson: "Man Running" and "Outrun the Constable"; *Adaptation:* Alma Reville; *Additional Dialogue:* James Bridie; *Director of Photography:* Wilkie Cooper; *Sets:* Terence Verity; *Music:* Leighton Lucas, conducted by Louis Levy; *Editing:* Edward Jarvis; *Sound Engineer:* Harold King; *Studio:* Elstree, G. B.; *Distributor:* Warner Brothers; *Principal Actors:* Marlene Dietrich (Charlotte Inwood), Jane Wyman (Eve Gill), Michael Wilding (Inspector Wilfred Smith), Richard Todd (Jonathan Cooper), Alastair Sim

(Commodore Gill), Dame Sybil Thorndike (Mrs. Gill), and Kay Walsh, Miles Malleson, Andre Morell, Patricia Hitchcock, Hector MacGregor, Joyce Grenfell.

STRANGERS ON A TRAIN / 1951
Production: Alfred Hitchcock, Warner Brothers, USA; *Screenplay:* Raymond Chandler and Czenzi Ormonde, from the novel by Patricia Highsmith; *Adaptation:* Whitfield Cook; *Director of Photography:* Robert Burks, ASC; *Special Photographic Effects:* H. F. Koene Kamp; *Sets:* Tec Hawortt and George James Hopkins; *Music:* Dimitri Tiomkin, conducted by Ray Heindorf; *Costumes:* Leah Rhodes; *Editing:* William H. Ziegler; *Sound Engineer:* Dolph Thomas; *Studio:* Warner Brothers; *Distributor:* Warner Brothers; *Principal Actors:* Farley Granger (Guy Haines), Ruth Roman (Ann Morton), Robert Walker (Bruno Anthony), Leo G. Carroll (Senator Morton), Patricia Hitchcock (Barbara Morton), Laura Elliot (Miriam Haines), Marion Lorne (Mrs. Anthony), Jonathan Hale (Mr. Anthony), and Howard St. John, John Brown, Norma Warden, Robert Gist, John Doucette, Charles Meredith, Murray Alper, Robert B. Williams, Roy Engel.

I CONFESS / 1952
Production: Alfred Hitchcock, Warner Brothers; *Associate Producer:* Barbara Keon; *Supervisory Producer:* Sherry Shourdes; *Screenplay:* George Tabori and William Archibald, from the play *Our Two Consciences* by Paul Anthelme; *Director of Photography:* Robert Burks, ASC; *Sets:* Edward S. Haworth and George James Hopkins; *Music:* Dimitri Tiomkin, conducted by Ray Heindorf; *Editing:* Rudi Fehr, ACE; *Costumes:* Orry-Kelly; *Sound Engineer:* Oliver S. Garretson; *Technical Consultant:* Father Paul la Couline; *Police Consultant:* Inspector Oscar Tangvay; *Studio:* Warner Brothers; *Location Work:* Quebec; *Assistant Director:* Don Page; *Distributor:* Warner Brothers; *Principal Actors:* Montgomery Clift (Father Michael Logan), Anne Baxter (Ruth Grandfort), Karl Malden (Inspector Larrue), Brian Aherne (Willy Robertson, the attorney), O. E. Hasse (Otto Keller), Dolly Haas (Alma Keller, his wife), Roger Dann (Pierre Grandfort), Charles André (Father Millais), Judson Pratt (Murphy, a policeman), Ovila Legare (Vilette, the lawyer), Giles Pelletier (Father Benoit).

DIAL M FOR MURDER / 1954
Production: Alfred Hitchcock, Warner Brothers; *Screenplay:* Frederick Knott, adapted from his stage play; *Director of Photography:* Robert Burks, ASC; *Film:* Naturalvision (3-D); *Color:* Warner Brothers, *Sets:* Edward Carrère and George James Hopkins; *Music:* Dimitri Tiomkin, conducted by composer; *Costumes:* Moss Marby; *Sound Engineer:* Oliver S. Garretson; *Editing:*

Rudi Fehr; *Studio:* Warner Brothers; *Distributor:* Warner Brothers; *Principal Actors:* Ray Milland (Tom Wendice), Grace Kelly (Margot Wendice), Robert Cummings (Mark Halliday), John Williams (Chief Inspector Hubbard), Anthony Dawson (Captain Swan Lesgate), Leo Britt (the narrator), Patrick Allen (Pearson), George Leigh (William), George Alderson (the detective), Robin Hughes (police sergeant).

REAR WINDOW / 1954
Production: Alfred Hitchcock, Paramount; *Screenplay:* John Michael Hayes, from a novelette by Cornell Woolrich; *Director of Photography:* Robert Burks, ASC; *Color:* Technicolor; *Consultant:* Richard Mueller; *Special Effects:* John P. Fulton; *Sets:* Hal Pereira, Joseph McMillan Johnson, Sam Comer, Ray Mayer; *Music:* Franz Waxman; *Editing:* George Tomasini; *Costumes:* Edith Head; *Assistant Director:* Herbert Coleman; *Sound Engineers:* Harry Lindgren and John Cope; *Distributor:* Paramount; *Principal Actors:* James Stewart (L. B. Jeffries, "Jeff"), Grace Kelly (Lisa Fremont), Wendell Corey (Thomas J. Doyle, the detective), Thelma Ritter (Stella, the nurse), Raymond Burr (Lars Thorwald), Judith Evelyn (Miss Lonelyheart), Ross Bagdasarian (the composer), Georgine Darcy (Miss Torse, the dancer), Jesslyn Fax (the lady sculptor), Rand Harper (honeymooner), Irene Winston (Mrs. Thorwald), and Denny Bartlett, Len Hendry, Mike Mahoney, Alan Lee, Anthony Warde, Harry Landers, Dick Simmons, Fred Graham, Edwin Parder, M. English, Kathryn Grandstaff, Havis Davenport.

TO CATCH A THIEF / 1955
Production: Alfred Hitchcock, Paramount; *Second Unit Direction:* Herbert Coleman; *Screenplay:* John Michael Hayes, from the novel by David Dodge; *Director of Photography:* Robert Burks, ASC (VistaVision); *Photography Second Unit:* Wallace Kelley; *Color:* Technicolor; *Consultant:* Richard Mueller; *Special Effects:* John P. Fulton; *Process Photo:* Farciot Edouart, ASC; *Sets:* Hal Pereira, Joseph MacMillian Johnson, Sam Comer, and Arthur Krams; *Music:* Lynn Murray; *Editing:* George Tomasini; *Costumes:* Edith Head; *Assistant Director:* Daniel McCauley; *Sound Engineers:* Lewis and John Cope; *Studio:* Paramount; *Principal Actors:* Cary Grant (John Robie), Grace Kelly (Frances Stevens), Charles Vanel (Bertrani), Jessie Royce Landis (Mrs. Stevens), Brigitte Auber (Danielle Foussard), Rene Blancard (Commissioner Lepic), and John Williams, Georgette Anys, Roland LeSaffre, Jean Hebey, Dominique Davray, Russel Gaige, Marie Stoddard, Frank Chellanok, Otto F. Schulze, Guy de Vestel, Bela Kovacs, John Alderson,

Don McGowan, W. Willie Davis, Edward Manouk, Jean Martinelli, Martha Bamattre, Aimee Torriani, Paul "Tiny" Newlan, Lewis Charles.

THE TROUBLE WITH HARRY / 1956
Production: Alfred Hitchcock, Paramount; *Screenplay:* John Michael Hayes, from the novel by John Trevor Story; *Director of Photography:* Robert Burks, ASC (VistaVision); *Special Effects:* John P. Fulton; *Color:* Technicolor; *Consultant:* Richard Mueller; *Sets:* Hal Pereira, John Goodman, Sam Comer, Emile Kuri; *Music:* Bernard Herrmann; *Song:* "Flaggin' the Train to Tuscaloosa"; *Lyrics:* Mack David; *Music:* Raymond Scott; *Editing:* Alma Macrorie; *Costumes:* Edith Head; *Studio:* Paramount; *Distributor:* Paramount; *Principal Actors:* Edmund Gwenn (Captain Albert Wiles), John Forsythe (Sam Marlowe, the painter), Shirley MacLaine (Jennifer, Harry's wife), Mildred Natwick (Miss Gravely), Jerry Mathers (Tony, Harry's son), Mildred Dunnock (Mrs. Wiggs), Royal Dano (Alfred Wiggs), and Parker Fennelly, Barry Macollum, Dwight Marfield, Leslie Wolff, Philip Truex, Ernest Curt Bach.

THE MAN WHO KNEW TOO MUCH (Second Version) / 1956
Production: Alfred Hitchcock, Paramount, Filmwite Productions; *Associate Producer:* Herbert Coleman; *Screenplay:* John Michael Hayes and Angus McPhail, from a story by Charles Bennett and D. B. Wyndham-Lewis; *Director of Photography:* Robert Burks, ASC; *Sets:* Hal Pereira, Henry Bumstead, Sam Comer, Arthur Krams; *Music:* Bernard Herrmann; *Lyrics:* Jay Livingston and Ray Evans: "Que Sera, Sera" ("Whatever Will Be"); "We'll Love Again"; "Storm Cloud Cantata" by Arthur Benjamin and D. B. Wyndham-Lewis, performed by the London Symphony Orchestra under the direction of Bernard Herrmann; *Editing:* George Tomasini, ACE; *Costumes:* Edith Head; *Sound Engineers:* Franz Paul and Gene Garvin, Western Electric; *Assistant Director:* Howard Joslin; *Studio:* Paramount; *Location Work:* Morocco, London; *Distributor:* Paramount; *Principal Actors:* James Stewart (Dr. Ben MacKenna), Doris Day (Jo, his wife), Daniel Gélin (Louis Bernard), Brenda de Banzie (Mrs. Drayton), Bernard Miles (Mr. Drayton), Ralph Truman (Inspector Buchanan), Mogens Wieth (the ambassador), Alan Mowbray (Val Parnell), Hilary Brooke (Jan Peterson), Christopher Olsen (little Hank MacKenna), Reggie Malder (Rien, the assassin), and Yves Brainville, Richard Wattis, Alix Talton, Noel Willman, Caroline Jones, Leo Gordon, Abdelhaq Chraibi, Betty Baskomb, Patrick Aherne, Louis Mercier, Anthony Warde, Lewis Martin, Richard Wordsworth.

THE WRONG MAN / 1957
Production: Alfred Hitchcock, Warner Brothers;
Associate Producer: Herbert Coleman; *Screenplay:*
Maxwell Anderson and Angus McPhail, from
"The True Story of Christopher Emmanuel
Balestrero" by Maxwell Anderson; *Director of
Photography:* Robert Burks, ASC; *Sets:* Paul
Sylbert and William L. Kuchl; *Music:* Bernard
Herrmann; *Editing:* George Tomasini; *Assistant
Director:* Daniel J. McCauley; *Studio:* Warner
Brothers; *Location Work:* New York; *Technical
Consultants:* Frank O'Connor (police magistrate
to the district attorney, Queens County, New
York); *Sound Engineer:* Earl Crain, Sr.; *Distributor:*
Warner Brothers; *Principal Actors:* Henry Fonda
(Christopher Emmanuel Balestrero—"Manny"),
Vera Miles (Rose, his wife), Anthony Quayle
(O'Connor), Harold J. Stone (Lt. Bowers), Charles
Cooper (Matthews, a detective), John Heldabrant
(Tomasini), Richard Robbins (Daniel, the guilty
man) and Esther Minciotti, Doreen Lang,
Laurinda Barrett, Norma Connolly, Nehemiah
Persoff, Lola D'Annunzio, Kippy Campbell, Robert
Essen, Dayton Lummis, Frances Reid, Peggy
Webber.

VERTIGO / 1958
Production: Alfred Hitchcock, Paramount;
Associate Producer: Herbert Coleman; *Screenplay:*
Alec Coppel and Samuel Taylor, from the novel
D'entre les Morts by Pierre Boileau and Thomas
Narcejac; *Director of Photography:* Robert Burks,
ASC (VistaVision); *Special Effects:* John Fulton;
Sets: Hal Pereira, Henry Bumstead, Sam Comer,
Frank McKelvey; *Color:* Technicolor; *Consultant:*
Richard Mueller; *Music:* Bernard Herrmann;
conducted by Muir Mathieson; *Editing:* George
Tomasini; *Costumes:* Edith Head; *Assistant
Director:* Daniel McCauley; *Sound Engineers:*
Harold Lewis and Winston Leverett; *Titles:* Saul
Bass; *Special Sequence:* Designed by John Ferren;
Studio: Paramount; *Location Work:* San Francisco;
Distributor: Paramount; *Principal Actors:* James
Stewart (John "Scottie" Ferguson), Kim Novak
(Madeleine Elster, Judy Barton), Barbara Bel
Geddes (Midge), Henry Jones (the coroner),
Tom Helmore (Gavin Elster), Raymond Bailey
(the doctor), and Ellen Corby, Konstantin Shayne,
Lee Patrick.

NORTH BY NORTHWEST / 1959
Production: Alfred Hitchcock, MGM; *Associate
Producer:* Herbert Coleman; *Original Screenplay:*
Ernest Lehman; *Director of Photography:* Robert
Burks, ASC (VistaVision); *Color:* Technicolor;
Consultant: Charles K. Hagedon; *Special
Photographic Effects:* A. Arnold Gillespie and
Lee Le Blanc; *Sets:* Robert Boyle, William A.
Horning, Merrill Pyle, Henry Grace, Frank
McKelvey; *Music:* Bernard Herrmann; *Editing:*
George Tomasini; *Title Design:* Saul Bass; *Sound

Engineer: Frank Milton; *Assistant Director:* Robert
Saunders; *Studio:* MGM; *Location Work:* New
York (Long Island), Chicago, Rapid City (Mount
Rushmore), South Dakota (National Memorial);
Distributor: Metro-Goldwyn-Mayer; *Principal Actors:*
Cary Grant (Roger Thornhill), Eva Marie Saint
(Eve Kendall), James Mason (Phillip Vandamm),
Jessie Royce Landis (Clara Thornhill), Leo G.
Carroll (the professor), Philip Ober (Lester
Townsend), Josephine Hutchinson (Mrs.
Townsend, the housekeeper), Martin Landau
(Leonard), Adam Williams (Valerian), and Carleton
Young, Edward C. Platt, Philip Coolidge, Doreen
Lang, Edward Binns, Robert Ellenstein, Lee
Tremayne, Patrick McVey, Ken Lynch, Robert B.
Williams, Larry Dobkin, Ned Glass, John
Bernardino, Malcolm Atterbury.

PSYCHO / 1960
Production: Alfred Hitchcock, Paramount;
Unit Manager: Lew Leary; *Screenplay:* Joseph
Stefano, from the novel by Robert Bloch;
Director of Photography: John L. Russel, ASC;
Special Photographic Effects: Clarence Champagne;
Sets: Joseph Hurley, Robert Claworthy, and
George Milo; *Music:* Bernard Herrmann; *Sound
Engineers:* Walden O. Watson and William Russell;
Title Design: Saul Bass; *Editing:* George Tomasini;
Assistant Director: Hilton A. Green; *Costumes:*
Helen Colvig; *Studio:* Paramount; *Principal Actors:*
Anthony Perkins (Norman Bates), Janet Leigh
(Marion Crane), Vera Miles (Lila Crane), John
Gavin (Sam Loomis), Martin Balsam (Milton
Arbogast, detective), John McIntire (Chambers,
the sheriff), Simon Oakland (Dr. Richmond), Frank
Albertson (the millionaire), Patricia Hitchcock
(Marion), and Vaughn Taylor, Lurene Tuttle,
John Anderson, Mort Mills.

THE BIRDS / 1963
Production: Universal; *Producer:* Alfred Hitchcock;
Screenplay: Evan Hunter, from the work by
Daphne du Maurier; *Director of Photography:*
Robert Burks, ASC; *Color:* Technicolor; *Special
Effects:* Lawrence A. Hampton; *Special Photo-
graphic Adviser:* Ub Iwerks; *Production Director:*
Norman Deming; *Sets:* Robert Boyle and George
Milo; *Sound Consultant:* Bernard Herrmann;
Composition and Production of Electronic Sound:
Remi Gassman and Oskar Sala; *Bird Trainer:*
Ray Berwick; *Assistant Director:* James H. Brown;
Assistant to Hitchcock: Peggy Robertson; *Illustrator:*
Alfred Whitlock; *Credits:* James S. Pollak; *Editing:*
George Tomasini; *Studio:* Universal; *Location
Work:* Bodega Bay, California; San Francisco;
Distributor: Universal; *Principal Actors:* Rod
Taylor (Mitch Brenner), Tippi Hedren (Melanie
Daniels), Jessica Tandy (Mrs. Brenner), Suzanne
Pleshette (Annie Hayworth), Veronica Cartwright
(Cathy Brenner), Ethel Griffies (Mrs. Bundy),
Charles McGraw (Sebastien Sholes), Ruth McDevitt

(Mrs. MacGruder), and Joe Mantell, Malcolm Atterbury, Karl Swenson, Elizabeth Wilson, Lonny Chapman, Doodles Weaver, John McGovern, Richard Deacon, Doreen Lang, Bill Quinn.

MARNIE / 1964

Production: Alfred Hitchcock, Universal; *Producer:* Albert Whitlock; *Screenplay:* Jay Presson Allen, from the novel by Winston Graham; *Director of Photography:* Robert Burks, ASC; *Color:* Technicolor; *Sets:* Robert Boyle and George Milo; *Music:* Bernard Herrmann; *Editing:* George Tomasini; *Assistant Director:* James H. Brown; *Assistant to Hitchcock:* Peggy Robertson; *Sound Engineers:* Waldon O. Watson and William Green; *Distributor:* Universal; *Principal Actors:* Tippi Hedren (Marnie Edgar), Sean Connery (Mark Rutland), Diane Baker (Lil Mainwaring), Martin Gabel (Sidney Strutt), Louise Latham (Bernice Edgar, Marnie's mother), Bob Sweeney (Cousin Bob), Alan Napier (Mr. Rutland), S. John Launer (Sam Ward), Mariette Hartley (Susan Clabon), and Bruce Dern, Henry Beckman, Edith Evanson, Meg Wyllie.

TORN CURTAIN / 1966

Producer: Alfred Hitchcock; *Assistant to Mr. Hitchcock:* Peggy Robertson; *Screenplay:* Brian Moore; *Director of Photography:* John F. Warren, ASC; *Sets:* Frank Arrigo; *Sound:* Walden O. Watson and William Russell; *Music:* John Addison; *Editing:* Bud Hoffman; *Assistant Director:* Donald Baer; *Principal Actors:* Paul Newman (Professor Michael Armstrong), Julie Andrews (Sarah Sherman), Lila Kedrova (Countess Kuchinska), Hans-jörg Felmy (Heinrich Gerhard), Tamara Toumanova (ballerina), Wolfgang Kieling (Hermann Gromek), Gunter Strack (Professor Karl Manfred), Ludwig Donath (Professor Gustav Lindt), David Opatoshu (Mr. Jacobi), Gisela Fischer (Dr. Koska), Mort Mills (farmer), Carolyn Conwell (farmer's wife), Arthur Gould-Porter (Freddy).

TOPAZ / 1969

Production: Alfred Hitchcock; *Assistant to Mr. Hitchcock:* Peggy Robertson; *Screenplay:* Samuel Taylor, from Leon Uris's novel; *Director of Photography:* Jack Hildyard; *Color:* Technicolor; *Sets:* John Austin, Alexander Golitzen, Henry Bumstead; *Costumes:* Edith Head (fashioned in Paris by Pierre Balongin); *Sound:* Waldron O. Watson, Robert R. Bertrand; *Editor:* William Ziegler; *Assistant Directors:* Douglas Green, James Westman; *Special Photographic Effects:* Albert Whitlock; *Music:* Maurice Jarre; *Studio:* Universal; *Location Work:* Copenhagen,

Wiesbaden, Paris, New York, Washington; *Principal Actors:* Frederick Stafford (Andre Devereaux), Dany Robin (Nicole Devereaux), Claude Jade (Michele Picard), Michel Subor (Francois Picard), Michel Piccoli (Jacques Granville), Philippe Noiret (Henri Jarré), John Forsythe (Michael Nordstrom), Karin Dor (Juanita de Cordoba), Per-Axel Arosenius (Boris Kusenov), Sonja Kolthoff (Mrs. Kusenov), John Vernon (Rico Parra), Roscoe Lee Browne (Philippe Dubois), Dan Randolph (Uribe), Tina Hedstrom (Tamara Kusenov), John Roper (Thomas), Anna Navarro (Carlotta Mendoza), Lewis Charles (Pablo Mendoza).

FRENZY / 1972

Producer: Alfred Hitchcock; *Assistant to Mr. Hitchcock:* Peggy Robertson; *Associate Producer:* William Hill; *Screenplay:* Anthony Shaffer, from the novel *Goodbye Piccadilly, Farewell Leicester Square* by Arthur Labern; *Production Manager:* Brian Burgess; *Assistant Director:* Colin M. Brewer; *Director of Photography:* Gil Taylor; *Special Photographic Effects:* Arthur Whitlock; *Editing:* John Jympson; *Sound:* Peter Handford, Gordon K. McCallum, Rusty Coppleman; *Music:* Ron Goodwin; *Color:* Eastman Color, CRI by Technicolor; *Production Design:* Sydney Cain; *Art Director:* Robert Laing; *Set Director:* Simon Wakefield; *Studio:* Pinewood, London; *Distributor:* Universal; *Principal Actors:* Jon Finch (Richard Blaney), Alec McCowen (Inspector Oxford), Barry Foster (Bob Rusk), Barbara Leigh-Hunt (Brenda Blaney), Anna Massey (Babs Milligan), Vivien Merchant (Mrs. Oxford), Billie Whitelaw (Hetty Porter), Bernard Cribbins (Felix Forsythe), Clive Swift (Johnny Porter), Michael Bates (Sergeant Spearman).

FAMILY PLOT / 1976

Production: Alfred Hitchcock; *Screenplay:* Ernest Lehman, from the novel *The Rainbird Pattern,* by Victor Canning; *Director of Photography:* Leonard J. South; *Assistant Director:* Howard Kazanjian; *Assistant to Mr. Hitchcock:* Peggy Robertson; *Art Director:* Henry Bumstead; *Set Decorator:* James Payne; *Production Illustrator:* Tom Wright; *Sound Mixer:* James Alexander; *Film Editor:* Terry Williams; *Special Effects:* Frank Brendel; *Music:* John Williams; *Costumes:* Edith Head; *Principal Actors:* Karen Black (Fran), Bruce Dern (Lumley), Barbara Harris (Madame Blanche), William Devane (Adamson), Cathleen Nesbitt (Julia Rainbird), Ed Lauter (Maloney), Katherine Helmond (Mrs. Maloney), and William Prince, Nicholas Colasanto, Louise Lorimer, Kate Murtagh, Clint Young, and Marge Redmond.

(Memory Shop)

Bibliography

Books

Harris, Robert A. And Michael Lasky. *The Films of Alfred Hitchcock.* Secaucus, New Jersey: Citadel Press, 1976.

Spoto, Donald. *The Art of Alfred Hitchcock.* New York: Doubleday & Co., Inc. 1979.

Taylor, John Russell. *Hitch.* New York: Pantheon Books, 1978.

Truffaut, François. *Hitchcock.* New York: Simon and Schuster, 1967.

Wood, Robin. *Hitchcock's Films.* New York: Castle Books, 1969.

Magazine Articles

Counts, Kyle, "The Birds." *Cinefantastique,* Fall 1980, pp. 15-35.

"Dial Ham for Murder." *Life,* May 24, 1954, pp. 92-107.

Hitchcock, Alfred. "The Woman Who Knew Too Much." *McCall's,* March 1956, p. 14.

"Hitchcock Speaking." *Cosmopolitan,* October 1956, pp. 43-50.

Martin, P. "I Call On Alfred Hitchcock." *Saturday Evening Post,* July 27, 1957, pp. 36-37.

Montagu, Ivor, "Working With Hitchcock." *Sight and Sound,* Summer 1980, pp. 189-193.

Index